By Benjamin Lewis

Published by:
Larstan Publishing, Inc., 10604 Outpost Dr.
N. Potomac MD, 20878
240-396-0007, ext. 901
www.larstan.com

PRINTED IN THE UNITED STATES OF AMERICA
10 9 8 7 6 5 4 3 2 1

Design and cover prints by Mike Gibson/Love Has No Logic Design Group
www.lovehasnologic.com

ISBN, Print Edition 978-0-9789182-1-7
Library of Congress Control Number: 2007935718
First Edition

PERFECTING THE PITCH

CREATING PUBLICITY THROUGH MEDIA RAPPORT

By Benjamin Lewis and a Sea of Media Professionals

Foreword By Former U.S. Congressman and U.S. Ambassador Richard N. Swett

TABLE OF CONTENTS

ACKNOWLEDGEMENTS

When I set out to write this book, I knew a moment would come when I would have to acknowledge everyone who has impacted me, my business and my life. Unfortunately, my publisher told me to keep this short, so I apologize in advance for missing anyone!

In my fifteen years as a publicist, I have learned a universal truth: No two publicists are the same. We all have different styles and different approaches. The important thing is to find your style and refine it every day, because the art of public relations is a creature that is always evolving.

I began to develop my style in college, while interning for former United States Congressman Richard Swett. It was there that I met Shireen Tilley, the congressman's chief of staff and press secretary, who took me "under her wing" and showed me the positive results respect for the media can produce. For that I am forever grateful.

I also want to thank my entire team at Perception, Inc.; they have taken it upon themselves to advance rapport-building with the media. Our clients are better off for the work Christen, Raj, Troy, Jessy, Wendy and Ashley do every day.

A special thanks to Kevin Adler, a good friend and outstanding journalist, who worked with me (tirelessly!) to make this book a reality. If not for his work, this book would be nothing more than a bunch of thoughts. He, more than anyone, is responsible for bringing the book to life. Thank you, Kevin!

I want to thank every journalist with whom I have had an opportunity to work over the years. People like Eileen Powell, Sharon Epperson, Paul Lim, Nicole Bullock, Lauren Young, Kim Lankford, Greg Greenberg, Richard Koreto, Marion Asnes and countless other journalists—consummate professionals all—helped me become the professional I am today.

To my family and friends, who stood by and watched as this book was being developed: I know many of you are saying, "I can't believe Ben wrote a book!!!" Well, now I have proof!

Finally to my wife, Wendy, thank you for supporting me in this endeavor. I know you believe in me and my dreams and aspirations. For that, I love you.

by Ambassador Richard N. Swett, FAIA

Andy Warhol once said we all will get our fifteen minutes of fame, but he wasn't thinking of Ben Lewis when he said that. *Perfecting The Pitch: Creating Publicity Through Media Rapport* is a well written, concise manual that helps you find ways to insure your "fame" lasts longer than fifteen minutes. How does he do it? Believe it or not, he does it by keeping the message simple, just like the pitch he is teaching us to craft. That is the beauty of this book; whether you are the owner of a small business with a meager marketing budget or the CEO of a substantial corporation, this book gives the kind of advice that is worthwhile for both users. Approachable yet substantive, Ben writes just like he advises, in a clear engaging way that is easy to follow.

As a former Member of Congress and Ambassador to Denmark, I am well aware of the need to have effective communicating skills. Whether you are promoting your business, your candidacy or your country, doing so effectively can mean the difference between initiating a deal, winning the election, or successfully negotiating the treaty or not. These successes are harder to achieve if you haven't created a favorable environment in which they can take place. To create that environment you need the "perfect pitch."

Ben is not a singer as far as I am aware but he has created his "perfect pitch" by drawing upon his experience and understanding accumulated over the years, starting with the work he did on my political campaigns just out of college. He now is the owner of a successful agency that helps clients apply what he has learned.

In his book, Ben starts out by describing a checklist of steps that will help any business owner to establish a clear description of the business. He then dedicates the remainder of the book to teaching how to use that information in "pitching" to the media in a way that will get the information published where customers will see it. Ben understands the importance of "free media" and that it comes from building relationships using his "pitch" method with members of the press.

Many books deal with issues of "branding" and communication, but this is the first book I have seen that focuses on helping the small business owner (and large business CEO) develop relationships with the press to enable the company to become better known.

To those who read this book, I can testify that the advice contained within these pages is tried and true, and with a little practice, anyone who uses these methods will improve their relationships with members of the media.

This book not only teaches how to structure the pitch, using the eight Content Rules outlined in Chapter 5, it goes on to offer a comprehensive national survey of journalists' preferences on how they should and should not be pitched to. This extremely useful information is followed by descriptions (quotes by actual reporters) of what works and doesn't work. Finally, the book concludes with the Principles of Public Relations, a comprehensive list of key ways to remember how to organize the creation of relationships with the media, identification of appropriate topics to pitch, structuring, presenting and following up on the pitch, and the wonderful results you will reap if you follow these guidelines. Anyone who reads this book will not only easily understand its message, but will be imbued with confidence to go out and immediately launch their own public relations campaign. Over time, you too will perfect your pitch.

With relationships with the press firmly established and a good story to tell, you will quickly see that your fifteen minutes of fame will be lengthened and the resulting benefit to your business will be significant.

Richard N. Swett, FAIA is a former Member of Congress, a former U.S. Ambassador to Denmark, President of Swett Associates, Senior Counselor at APCO Worldwide, and author of the book, *Leadership by Design: Creating an Architecture of Trust*. He provides Vision Leadership on large, complex development projects.

The Kato Syndrome

> ## I'm not just going to fade out, I know
> ### —Brian "Kato" Kaelin

People crave attention. They seek it in many ways and for any number of reasons. For many people, moments in the spotlight are short-lived. Even worse, their attempts at achieving notoriety are seen for what they actually are—ego gratification. As we learned in the early 1990s from Kaelin, a once-famous L.A. houseguest, getting attention is easy. Keeping it—and earning the respect of the media and the public—is something completely different.

Too many people want the attention of the media, but lack the substance to create long-lasting relationships with journalists. And these failures are not just broken-down actors caught in the spotlight, like Kato Kaelin; they come from every industry and profession. They make spectacles of themselves, and sometimes their displays do generate short-term attention. But in the end, their efforts generate very little substance. I call this the "Kato Syndrome."

Andy Warhol termed this syndrome "Fifteen Minutes of Fame" for good reason. Warhol wisely recognized that people and fads quickly move in and out of favor. In today's voracious media market, the ability to get those fifteen minutes might be easier than ever, but the challenge to keep the media's attention has increased even more significantly. Celebrities flame out quickly (Does anyone care to remember rapper Vanilla Ice or Jennifer Wilbanks, the "Runaway Bride?"), but so do business celebrities. Hundreds of pretenders had their moments in the sun, then quickly faded into obscurity.

Managing your public relations outreach can help you avoid the fate of the flashes-in-the-pan. By building a reputation based on substance, not flash, you will be able to sustain the positive attention of the media. By generating the respect of individual reporters and editors, you will become a valued source of news and analysis upon whom reporters rely repeatedly.

It Takes Passion

Your competence is at the core of building respect and rapport with the media, but it takes more than competence. Passion is the other key ingredient in a mutually beneficial relationship with the media.

Fortunately, as a business owner and entrepreneur, you probably already have great passion for what you do. In working with owners, entrepreneurs and other professionals and experts, I have seen the power of the passionate approach. Without exception, these leaders are passionate about what they do. (Why else would they be doing what they are doing?!). Their passion is infectious; leaders prompt people to believe in what they are saying and selling.

Deepak Chopra and his writings on spirituality; Tony Robbins and his work as a motivational speaker and life coach; and Zig Ziglar and his work on business and leadership development have helped them each develop cult-like followings because of passion. Sure, their ideas and belief systems resonate with people; that's the substance of their messages. But if you see them speak, you quickly realize that their passion creates the real connections with their audiences.

Your passion sells your products, services and ideas. Think about the last time you sat through a sales pitch for a product or service you may have been considering. Was the person presenting to you passionate, excited and informed? Did he or she make you feel that the product was the best possible solution for you and your needs? How the person presented the product was as influential as the product itself.

I am well into my second decade as a public relations professional, and I have dozens of clients in the financial services business. My clients and I have endured enough changes in market conditions to last a lifetime. We rode high during the dot-com bubble economy of the late 1990s; we struggled with panicked investors when the market downturn began in 2000 and was worsened by 9/11; and we tried to explain the origins of the rebound of the past few years.

Through these business cycles, I have seen the media adopt and discard hundreds of storylines: Boom and Bust, Exuberance and Collapse.

For each era, we developed a specific message, or set of messages that spoke to the issues foremost in the minds of investors. During the dot-com boom, we reminded people that the extraordinarily good times could not last forever. During the market correction, we focused on making good long-term decisions. During the remarkable resurgence, we praised America's economic resiliency, but we also warned that the housing market was showing some of the same bubble-like signs that the dot-coms did just a few years earlier. Each of these messages was consistent with the big-picture principles of responsible investing that my clients wanted to portray.

Through it all, I have counseled my clients that, while they cannot control events, they can control how they want to present their stories. They need to be consistent in their approaches and honest at all times. They must develop their storylines (their brand identities), and stick with them. They must also be sure that the media and the general public know what they stand for, and that they are passionate about their beliefs.

My clients approach the art of selling every day. Good ideas and deep knowledge are critical. But it's just as critical that they come across as excited about what they are doing. The business owner who is passionate will generate passion in the media (and in his or her clients, as well).

Keep this in mind…content is important, but passion sells. It doesn't matter if you are presenting an idea, a product or a service. It doesn't matter if you are talking to a client or customer, a prospect, a business partner or a member of the media. If you are passionate about what you are offering, your audience will buy into it.

This is what separates people like Kato Kaelin from Tony Robbins. Knowledge, experience, content and passion give people staying power. They grow their opportunities with the media into effective, long-term relationships. The ideas in this book are only going to work if you have the passion.

Make members of the media believe in you, and you will have far more than fifteen minutes of fame!

CHAPTER 1

It's About Rapport

Building a business is all about developing and maintaining strong relationships. You work every day to strengthen your relationships with your customers, your staff, your suppliers and your peers. You strive to be known as innovative, trustworthy and expert — in short, to be recognized as a leader in your field.

How to Build Rapport

To build rapport with a reporter, do things that help him or her do their job.

- Be a source of ideas. The pressure is immense on reporters to find something new and different. You can turn that to your advantage by becoming a source of ideas for a time-pressed reporter who has to provide his editor with three great story ideas at Monday's editorial meeting.

- Provide a variety of sources to contact.

- Provide objective data.

- Return a reporter's calls and emails, even if you don't have information to share on the topic.

You should devote the same effort to building a relationship with the media. Your goal should be to become a resource of timely, accurate and relevant information. If you deliver consistently, you will reap the benefits. Not only will you gain new customers, but they will approach with a positive impression of you already in place just from what they've seen and read about you in publications and broadcast programs.

Media coverage provides businesses with billions of dollars of free promotion each year.

Perfecting The Pitch by Benjamin Lewis

The World Association of Newspapers reported in June 2006 that 439 million people in 210 countries buy a newspaper every day. The Association of Publishing Agencies reported in July 2006 that 1.4 billion magazines are purchased every year. Television, radio and Web viewership dwarf those numbers. It all adds up to an extraordinary number of opportunities for you to make a positive impression on prospective customers. And the best part is you don't have to have special skills to make that positive impression. You just have to be able to talk about what you do best.

Whatever business you are in, there are media outlets eager to share news of your activities with their readers. The media is in the business of educating and entertaining its audience, and it looks to you for the expertise and the content. This is true for "new media" web sites and bloggers just as much as it is true for "old media" newspapers, magazine, television and radio.

But you won't be able to tap into this river of opportunity unless you first lay the groundwork. You must establish and maintain credibility with reporters and editors you contact. You must be available when they need your help. You must be able to speak on the key issues of the day in your industry or profession.

While the reporters need you, they have an overwhelming number of other business people and experts also seeking their attention. In every field, the competition for media coverage is getting tougher. You need to demonstrate why you should be selected from among the crowd. You need to be more attractive than the competition.

Your rapport with individual reporters, journalists and editors is at the heart of your media success. Rapport is a fancy word for trust, respect, familiarity — and relationships.

How do you build strong relationships?

Right Place at the Right Time

Building rapport takes time and effort. It takes being at the right place at the right time. Better yet, it's about being at the right place even before it's the right time.

Here's how rapport worked for two entrepreneurs.

THE OIL SPILL EXPERT

During the 1970s and 1980s, Richard Golob amassed the world's most extensive data base about oil spills. He had a small client base of oil companies, but the impact of his work — and the size of his business — were quite limited.

Instead of just sitting on the oil spill information, Golob maintained a regular flow of short reports to mass media journalists who covered environmental issues or the oil industry. He developed a proprietary list of the largest oil spills, which he allowed newspapers and magazines to reprint. He shared information on the environmental effects of spills and development of new cleanup technology.

When the Exxon Valdez oil tanker went aground off the coast of Alaska in 1989, all the major television networks and metropolitan newspapers needed an oil spill expert who didn't work for the oil companies. They came to Richard Golob. He became a regular on network TV and the Cable News Network (CNN).

The attention paid off. Golob's consulting business quadrupled, and he was invited to make speeches at dozens of conferences. He was hired to provide technical assistance on several Valdez documentaries, and was tapped by a major textbook publisher to write The Almanac of Science and Technology.

THE 401(K) GURU

In 1989, Michael Scarborough, MBA, began to focus his financial advisory practice on helping individuals use their 401(k) plans most effectively. In working with hundreds (and then thousands) of individuals, he realized that people were putting their retirement savings at greater risk than they realized by concentrating assets in the investments that offered the highest possible returns. People seemed to ignore the greater risks they were taking in what were supposed to be safe, long-term accounts.

In the late 1990s during the high-tech investment craze, Scarborough found an unprecedented number of people were placing all their faith in their employers' stocks. It was common for people to commit 10 percent of their 401(k) portfolio to their company stock. Basically, they were doubling-up their risk, because if their company struggled, they would not only lose on their investments, but they might lose their jobs.

Understanding that concentrated blocks of stocks were the riskiest possible investment – especially for 50-year-old telecom employees – Scarborough pressed his case to the media. He wanted the media's help in getting the word out. He believed that people were foolishly placing their lives in the hands of their employers. But few members of the media listened.

Then came Enron, Lucent and WorldCom.

Overnight, Scarborough's phone began to ring. The mainstream financial news media realized that his recommendation to invest no more than 5 percent of a 401(k) in an employer's stock was good advice. Scarborough spoke on national television and national and local radio, as well as granting scores of interviews to magazines and newspapers. The fact that Scarborough knew thousands of participants at some of the biggest U.S. companies added to his credibility. He understood how companies' retirement plans worked, while being independent of plans themselves.

As his standing as a 401(k) guru solidified, Scarborough wrote two popular books that outlined his investment strategies. Individuals and institutions continue to flock to him for advice and counsel.

Mastering the Media Pitch

This book will teach you all the elements for being in the right place at the right time and for mastering the media pitch. First, the book will explain the techniques for developing "pitch-friendly" messages. Next, it will show you how to identify the media members most receptive to your message. Finally, the book will give you insights into the minds and motivations of real journalists on the receiving end of media pitches every day, so that you can ensure that your pitch gets right to the heart of what they are seeking.

However, all this advice is useless if you don't have rapport with the news media in the first place. Unless you have already laid the groundwork to become a trusted source, then your ideas will just be clutter on the computers and voicemails of journalists. You will be wasting your time and theirs. Worse yet, when a journalist is seeking an expert on a topic, you will see your competitors being quoted instead of you. They have invested in establishing a working relationship with the media.

Put yourself in the position of a reporter working in the print or electronic media world today. It's a fast-paced, high-stress environment. Reporters get dozens or even hundreds of pitches and press releases each week. They can only follow up on a few. They will always go with the person they know (and trust) over an unknown. A reporter does not want to make a highly public mistake by working with an unreliable source. Even if an unknown person has impressive-sounding credentials, the reporter will need to test that person's reliability on small issues before being confident about using him or her as a major source.

You have to break through the clutter of press releases and set yourself apart from the pack. Fortunately, as Chapter 2 shows, you can use many of the same brand identification techniques that drive your business to forge strong relationships with key media figures.

Your brand is built upon the quality of your message, the passion with which you present it and the integrity that you display. Just as these attributes create a strong relationship with your customers and prospects, they create a rapport with the media. Think of it as your marketing campaign to recruit the media as your customer.

Media as Your Target Audience

If you think about marketing to the media, you begin by identifying your universe of possible buyers and then narrowing in on your most likely customers. You study that sub-group and understand what it values, and what motivates it to act. You make sure that your product

Proactive vs. Reactive PR: One Leads to the Other

I hear it from every new client.... "I want to be the first and only resource a member of the media ever uses. When they need something answered on my specialty, I want them to think of me!"

I'm supposed to be able to deliver on this goal with a few well-chosen phrases and inside connections. But I have to break the news to new clients and prospects that their ambitions will not become reality unless they take the initiative. They must support my efforts to make them known to the media through a process that I call Proactive PR.

You need to reach out to the media. Tell them who you are, what you do, what you provide your customers or clients, and why you are unique. Journalists already have their stable of trusted sources, and you need to convince them to add you to that "A List" and that Rolodex.

meets its needs, and that you can explain why your product is the best choice. Finally, you contact the audience with a clear, concise message emphasizing how your product satisfies those needs.

Here's how a media campaign puts those concepts into practice. First, you start by deciding which media members to target. The logical place to start is with the publications and other media outlets that you rely on for news. What do you read? What do you listen to or watch? Who are the opinion leaders in your industry? Your geographic area? Your desired audience? Which reporters, columnists and commentators do you respect, and why?

Next, think about what those opinion leaders care about. What topics do they cover? How do they cover them? Do they write lengthy, detailed articles with a lot of numbers and data? Do they write shorter pieces? Do they use humor? Do they look for stories with a harder

Pitching is the heart of Proactive PR. Over time, you demonstrate your expertise and knowledge through the act of pitching, and you gradually become a trusted source, a go-to person, a member of the "A List."

Pitching means sharing timely, newsworthy story ideas with reporters who actively cover your industry. The more ideas you can formulate the more of a resource you become. Make sure these ideas relate to your brand, your skills and your message. Think about stories and anecdotes that prove your point. Show how your ideas are worth money to the journalist's audience.

After you've been proactive and proven your value, journalists will start to call you. That's what I call Reactive PR. At that point, through your regular contacts with the media, you can continue to present information to both target audiences. You and the journalist have established rapport. You are in a partnership of sorts—exchanging the information that he finds valuable for the access that benefits you.

edge or controversy, or are they more apt to write about topics with more general interest?

Next, assess which aspects of your business are most relevant to these opinion leaders. What do you do best that will appeal to each of their areas of interest? You can segment your approach, just as you would with customers and prospects, because different media members look for different issues. But you still want to keep in mind your overall brand strengths and ensure that all discussions reflect some aspect of those strengths.

Finally, reach out to the media through *media* pitches. Later chapters in this book will give you concrete examples of pitch formats, pitch cycles and schedules, and specific do's and don'ts from an exclusive survey of today's working media.

Use this framework to launch your public relations campaign. Work through these types of questions to anticipate what is valuable to your target media and create what I call Proactive PR. Through those efforts, you can bring your knowledge and perspective to the media in a timely, usable format so they can share your expertise with their audience.

Pitching and Rapport

While successful pitching comes after rapport has been developed, the good news is that pitching helps build rapport over time, too. When you make a good pitch, you are showing a member of the media that you're an expert on topics of interest to a reporter and that you are eager to share that information with his audience. You are offering to help him do his job more effectively.

Information is the "currency" of the news business; it's what newspapers, magazines, web sites and television provide to their customers, readers and viewers. It's not too different than the way your business operates, except maybe your business sells insurance and your "currency" is your expertise in insurance policies, life expectancies and tax issues.

You want to generate good transactions with the media, just as you do with your customers. In every good transaction, each of the participants gets something he or she needs, often leading to long-term working relationships. For a reporter, a successful transaction comes from working with a source that is helpful, understands deadlines and is honest. That's the type of person that a reporter will contact again.

The U.S. Supreme Court in 2005 issued a ruling in Kelo v. City of New London that expanded the ability of states to take land from private citizens through eminent domain. The case had not been high on the business community's radar screen.

But one law firm was not surprised. When the Court said it would take the case, the firm sent story pitches to dozens of publications explaining the potential significance of the case, and alerting reporters and editors to the upcoming Supreme Court oral arguments. A few publications took note with brief news items, but none was ready at the time to explore the issue in depth.

Then the ruling was announced, and it surprised the real estate development community and local and state legislators. The law firm immediately contacted reporters and offered to share its expertise, building on its previous pitches. Within a week, the law firm was the primary resource for more than a dozen legal trade journals and real estate development business newspapers. Its partners made many a front page, providing analysis of the ruling and explanations of its possible impact. Within a few weeks, the firm had arranged meetings with several multi-billion-dollar developers that wanted to discuss the implications for their properties.

The firm continues to consult with property owners across the country, while states are rewriting their laws in response to the Supreme Court opinion.

Why Work with the Media?

Before going further in this book, you might want some assurance that working with the media is actually beneficial. After all, developing and sustaining regular media contact can be a time-consuming and difficult task.

Pitching is certainly more difficult than just paying for traditional advertising, Yellow Pages listings or other promotions. Also, with traditional advertising, you get complete control of your message because you write your own copy. With pitching, you cannot ultimately control what someone writes or says.

In a pitch, you are asking the media to cover a topic in a way that you feel is appropriate, but you have to accept that the reporter and editor have final judgment. You might give a reporter a great idea and provide details for an article, only to discover your point is buried near the end. You might not even be quoted in the final product, or you might find an interpretation that does not completely support your viewpoint. That's the risk you take when you make a news pitch. Reporters and editors are independent-minded; you cannot dictate their messages.

So why should you take the less direct, more complicated route of a pitch? Why should you work with the media when the outcome is uncertain? Let's explore four very good reasons.

First, the media provides you a high-profile forum to display your expertise and knowledge. This is crucial to building a successful and sustainable business because ultimately, you are selling your knowledge. To give your company every chance to succeed, you need to take advantage of every avenue available to publicize your skills.

Even in this era of blogs and online video, the mainstream media remains a powerful tool for bringing your unique insight to the public's attention. Magazine and newspaper publishers command the attention of thousands, tens of thousands, or even millions of readers, depending on the publication. Television can reach tens of millions of people. These are tremendous sources for generating publicity and strengthening your brand image.

Don't think of pitching and PR as substitutes for advertising and marketing. Think of them as complements.

Second, the impact of media coverage you receive is compounded many-fold because the media has unique credibility with your customer base and the public at large. Customers and prospects who see you in print or hear you on a radio program will perceive your company or organization more positively. You benefit from the credibility that the media outlet has built over years or decades — and the reputation that the publication has for staying on top of news and ahead of trends.

Magazine readers or radio listeners also understand that their favorite media outlet has made a decision that you and your company are leaders in your field. You have been "vetted" to some degree by the gatekeepers of information: reporters and editors. The approval of these gatekeepers signals to customers and prospects that you are credible and your expertise is worthwhile. Think about how many times you have had this reaction: If that person is good enough to be interviewed, then he must be an expert.

Of course, you could get into the same media outlets through paid advertising. But everyone knows that content comes from the company to make a company look good. Interviews and feature stories in a publication or on the radio or TV are known to be much more objective.

Third, media appearances provide you with additional material for marketing campaigns. Whenever you are quoted in the newspaper, you should send an e-mail to your customers to draw their attention to your comments. If you are going to be on television, send a message in advance of the program and encourage people to watch the show.

After your media appearance, use it to present yourself in the best possible light to prospective customers and clients. If you were featured in a magazine article or on a "Best Of …" list in your business or profession, purchase copies of the article and make them part of your marketing package for prospects. If you were on radio or TV, make an attractive, glossy flier that reprints some of your quotes and include your photo and information on the media appearance. If it's possible, create electronic links from your web site to the media's online article, too.

Fourth, if your current customers see the organization as a frequently used resource, they will feel even more strongly that they have made a good decision to work with you. People are pleased to be affiliated with highly recognized, highly credible organizations.

Positive and regular references in the media will help you retain your customers and will encourage those customers to provide you with referrals for more business.

Conclusion

In this opening chapter, we've discussed the importance of building rapport with members of the media. You provide the media with ideas and information that will satyisfy readers and viewers, and the media shares your expertise with a broad audience. This win-win relationship is an extremely powerful complement to any company's marketing efforts; in fact, it can generate opportunities far beyond anything that traditional advertising and marketing can produce.

The best public relations campaigns begin with a thorough understanding of what you are and what competitive advantages you possess. The effort is supported by a passion for your work and commitment to make yourself known to the world. But passion and commitment will not take you far if you don't have a powerful brand identity to bring to your media contacts. In the next chapter, we will help you discover and define your brand identity.

CHAPTER 2

Defining Your Brand: The N+I+R=S$_2$ Equation

A good rapport with news media enables you to get out your message. But what message do you want to present? Your message comes from brand identity, or what we call your "Verbal Brand."

Brands can take many forms. Visual brands, such as famous logos and instantly recognizable color palates, probably first come to mind. The McDonald's golden arches and the Nike swoosh are examples that every other business owner envies for their familiarity.

Businesses spend millions of dollars annually to capture the perfect Visual Brand. Too often, they go about it the wrong way. Visual Brands need to represent a message the company is trying to communicate — a message identified in a Verbal Brand. If the Verbal Brand is ignored, a company is, unfortunately, putting the cart before the horse.

Your Verbal Brand highlights the best attributes of your business. It's a challenging task to put this into a few words, but the effort will bring great rewards.

Branding has been a powerful tool for businesses for more than a century, but it's never been more important than today. Each of us is highly brand-conscious, and we rely on brands to help us select from among a remarkable array of choices. Most likely, there are dozens or even thousands of other entrepreneurs fighting for the same exposure in newspapers and on radio, the Web and TV. What specialties set you apart? Do you serve a particular niche? Identify your uniqueness and use it as your portal into the media. You can turn branding to your advantage if you're instantly recognized by your customer base for what you do best.

Your brand is captured in the $N+I+R=S_2$ Equation. This equation summarizes how your Name, Image and Reputation add up to your brand image. Bring them together seamlessly and you'll achieve your ultimate goal: Success.

Let's look at these elements individually.

Name

Your company's name is more than just the words on your business card and letterhead. Your name identifies who you are, what you stand for and who you serve.

If your name is well selected and you maintain a consistent message, you will generate a positive reaction with your target audience. When prospects and customers see your name over time, they will associate it with the best attributes about your company and when they come to you, they will feel as if they already know you. They have pre-selected you and your business because of who and what you are. You are well on your way to having them as a client or a customer.

All of us are familiar with hundreds of brand names: Nike, McDonald's, The Wall Street Journal, Federal Express, Coca-Cola, Microsoft, Wal-Mart, Walt Disney and so on. Every one of these names evokes a clear image of what the companies do, what products and services they provide and what principles they stand for. These companies are standard-bearers in their fields, and whether we give them our money or not, we are always making an implicit comparison between what they offer and what else is available.

The best-known brand names have another lesson to share with us. In many cases, the actual names of these brands do not directly identify what the company does. Walt Disney is named after its founder; it does not identify itself as a filmmaker or theme park dynasty. McDonald's does not have the terms "hamburgers and fries" in its title. Nike was the Greek goddess of victory; and while that suggests athletic endeavors, it's doubtful that most Americans make the association with mythology today.

So how do these companies build their name recognition when their names do not immediately bring to mind their businesses? They use a **tagline.** A tagline is a short, memorable phrase that either adds important factual details or generates a positive emotional response. Examples of effective taglines include:

Nike: *Just Do It*
GE: *We Bring Good Things to Light*
CitiGroup: *Live Richly*
Merrill Lynch: *Bullish on America*
Federal Express: *When It Absolutely, Positively Has To Be There Overnight*

Taglines focus on what makes a company superior, special and trustworthy. In my years working with financial advisors and entrepreneurs, I have found taglines are as effective for companies serving specific market niches as they are for world-famous multinational corporations.

Developing Your Verbal Brand Name

Think of your firm's name and tagline as your Verbal Brand. The short, memorable phrase will quickly give a potential customer or a member of the media an understanding of who you are, what you do and which attributes set you apart from the competition.

Don't settle for generalities in a Verbal Brand. Too many firms take the easy approach, with vague and tired phrases.

The financial services industry, for example, is rife with promises to "provide comprehensive financial planning," "offer a client-centered approach" or "work with high net worth individuals."

These firms would be better positioned if they used more descriptive and detailed phrases. Customers would have a greater understanding of what the firm does if they were greeted by phrases such as:

- "We revisit our clients' investments twice a year to make sure they're appropriately distributed."

- "We walk our clients through the ins and outs of estate planning."

- "We conduct comprehensive, ongoing estate planning for families with a minimum net worth of $5 million."

Begin to create a Verbal Brand by conducting a self-analysis. This is not an easy task, and you'll need to set aside time to do it well. You'll need to involve your entire staff, and you'll need to solicit feedback from some clients. Yet, the time and effort will pay great dividends.

The process begins by answering six sets of questions to help identify benefits you provide to customers. From this large mass of qualities, focus on a few that best reflects your vision of the company. These strengths will then help you create several Verbal Brands and taglines. Ask your clients which is the most meaningful to them. Then use that feedback to finalize your Verbal Brand and start using it to define yourself to the outside world, including the media.

1. **Who, what, when, where, why?**

   Who are you? Describe in a few sentences the professions of the principals of your business.

   What do you do? Answering this question requires careful balance. How you define your business has an impact on what you do and how you are perceived. You do not want to be so specific that you exclude potential customers, but you do not want to be so general that your description is meaningless.

   For example, an accounting firm would say it offers accounting services. But it must go deeper. Does the firm do individual tax returns? Does it do business tax returns? Does it specialize in certain types of businesses?

Where do you do it? For many businesses, a geographic focus is a crucial part of their identity. They build deep roots in a community and prosper because they know their market so well. If this describes your business, make sure that your Verbal Brand states it as clearly as possible. For example, Big Apple Party Supply is a better Verbal Brand than Mega-Party Supply, if the business truly focuses on New York City.

Conversely, one of the primary mistakes that small companies make in their Verbal Brand is to come up with a name that is well beyond their actual ambitions. Universal Dog Training or International Florists probably do not convey the warmth and familiarity that locally-based businesses really want to present.

On the other hand, if the business is truly serving a national or international audience, then that should be clearly stated. Many small consulting businesses, for example, should be wary about using a name that understates their scope and reach, if they truly are able to work worldwide.

When are you a good fit? Similar to defining what you do, this question forces you to focus on who you serve. Few, if any, businesses can serve all people all the time. McDonald's does not position itself as the place for a romantic dinner or an expense-account lunch meeting.

Why would someone use you? Define the benefits you provide prospective customers. Make sure that these are identified from the perspective of the client or customer and not the company.

2. Credentials

Education/Degrees. In many businesses, your degrees and education matter greatly. Yours may serve as a shorthand message that you received a great foundation to work in this field.

Designations/Certifications. Which credentials really matter in your field? Do the principals in your firm have them? Does your prospective client base understand those credentials, or will you have to explain them?

Experience. How long have you been in this line of work? How does that demonstrate your capabilities? Often, it is valuable to include a reference to your business' years of experience into the tagline if it can demonstrate credibility, stability and know-how.

Professional Affiliations. Which professional organizations have you joined? Do you hold a leadership role in any of them?

Exposure. Have you been named to a "Best of" list in your field or region? These types of third-party commendations carry great weight with prospective clients and the media.

Strategic Partnerships. Are you affiliated with well-known organizations, either in your field or in related fields? Can you leverage their exposure to build your own?

3. **Target Audience**

Perception of Your Intended Audience. Who should you target? Define this in a way that truly drives your business operations and marketing strategy. If you are a car repair shop, don't say that your target audience is every driver in your state. That is so broad that it's not helpful. Most likely, your customers are drawn from close by, as they want the convenience of dropping off a car near home. Also, you probably have expertise in several car makes or models. So your primary target audiences are people within a certain geographic region who drive certain types of cars.

Current clients and customers. A great reality check for most businesses is to find out about their current clients and customers. Do they represent the same people you're targeting? In which ways do they differ?

You can learn about your customers through many methods. A quick way is to review sales records. Using the example of the car repair shop, read the repair orders to identify most customers' ZIP code, types of cars brought in and problems most frequently fixed. For businesses that have mailing lists, a geographic analysis can be quick.

You also can conduct a survey of customers in order to get greater detail. Write a survey on no more than both sides of one sheet of paper that asks relevant questions to help you gauge your business.

For consumer-oriented businesses, your survey will typically ask your customers' age, income level, gender, education level, professions and location. In the case of a car repair shop, a customer's education level or profession is perhaps not very important. But a person's location, car makes and models are very relevant. For a financial advisor, a client's income and investing experience may be the most important pieces of information.

Your survey should also ask a few questions about what product or service customers are seeking from you, and whether they are satisfied with what they receive.

4. Services/Products

What services do you offer? Start by making a list of all the things that you can provide customers. This broad list gives you insight into your business's full potential scope – and limitations.

What services are you actually performing? Now, look at the list of services you offer, especially those that customers are not requesting. Why? Do customers know about them? Do customers not need them? Are they priced competitively?

Ultimately, you may decide to re-emphasize services that are not being utilized. If you are confident that those services will be desired, retain them in your branding model. However, you primarily should focus on what you are actually doing, rather than what you aspire to do several years from now.

Share of time on each service. Rank the services you provide from most to least frequent. You should be aware that whatever tops your list is likely to be how your customers, prospects and the media view you. If you want to change their perceptions, you will have to work hard.

Which services provide the greatest revenue? Now make another list of your services, but rank them by greatest revenue potential. You might be surprised to find that the work you spend the most time on is not the most profitable. Are you satisfied with the current distribution of services you provide, or are you hoping that your media outreach campaign can bring in new customers who will want your more value-added services? This question has a significant impact on your final Verbal Brand.

5. **Benefits**

This is often the most difficult part of the exercise for entrepreneurs. You must look at your company from your clients' perspectives. Building on the products and services identified in the previous exercise, rank all of the benefits that you provide from the most-valued to the least-valued, but from their perspective. This will tell you what you really are.

The process is called "force-ranking," and many marketing and public relations firms use it with their clients. The variation on force-ranking shown below (developed by Vestment Advisors, a business consulting firm in Minneapolis) has proven to be quite effective in helping businesses identify their true customer benefits. Vestment says what's most important for a business is to provide those benefits their customers most strongly desire. Focusing on these identified benefits can help any business break through barriers that prevent growth.

Vestment Advisors suggests creating a list of every perceived benefit you offer your clients and customers. If a benefit is broad, drill down to identify the sub-benefits.

Once the list is developed, force-rank each item against every other item. Force-ranking means that every item is placed in the correct location on the priority list. This can be a challenging exercise if you provide 50, 60 or even 70 benefits, which is not uncommon.

Here is how force-ranking might work for a financial services firm:

Acme Financial Services, Inc. Benefits Force Ranking
1. Customer service
2. Integrity
3. Detailed financial plan development
4. Monthly phone calls to discuss status
5. Access to a large menu of investment vehicles
6. Independence
7. Fee-only compensation
8. 30 years of investment experience
9. Provides comprehensive planning (looks at every aspect of financial well-being)
10. Quarterly newsletters

To conduct a force-ranking exercise, Acme Financial would get all of its employees together and ask them to step into the shoes of the firm's clients. The staff would look at the first two items on the list and decide which is more important to the client. Is it "customer service" or "integrity"? Once everyone votes for their favorite, a mark is placed next to the preferred benefit. Then the first item is considered against the third item on the list. Which is more important—"customer service" or "detailed financial plan development"? A mark is placed next to the preferred benefit. The entire list is completed this way, comparing "customer service" to every other benefit. Once this has been done for Item No. 1, the same procedure is followed to force-rank Item No. 2 against the other items on the list. The exercise is completed for the entire list.

Once done, count how many marks are next to each item. The four highest vote-getters will become the foundation for the Verbal Brand.

b. Competition

Who are your closest competitors? Before completing the exercise, you need to look outside of your company. Your customers are surely considering your competitors before making a purchasing decision, so you need to be aware of who you're up against.

What do they offer? Your competitors probably offer some services or products that differ from yours. You should identify those differences, as well as the areas in which you directly compete.

How are you superior? Identify what sets you apart from your competitors. Figure out how that compares with the products and services your customers say they value most highly. Are you providing those highest-value items, or are your competitors?

The Verbal Brands

With this self-survey completed, you are well on your way to developing or enhancing your Verbal Brand. It will flow through several types of messages that you develop and use repeatedly in your communications. These include your core messages and personal story that are then summarized in your "elevator statement" and tagline.

CORE MESSAGES (ACES)

Your core messages are the absolute best things you can say about your firm. I refer to these as your Aces, because they are the equivalent of holding four aces in your hand in a poker game; you can't do better.

You've already determined your strengths and cross-referenced them with what clients and customers value most highly. Now you need to pick from the top-ranked to mold your messages. There is no ideal number of Aces, but experience indicates that three, four or five are usually most effective.

These Aces must be focused on your firm. They must be positive. They must be easily understood. They should be broad enough to appeal to a fairly wide customer base, yet differentiate from the claims direct competitors can make.

Common Aces are: integrity; professionalism; experience; client service; trust; dependability; range of services; and superior communications. You need to be able to back up each Ace with a specific example about your company. For example, an accounting firm that uses experience as an Ace might have three CPAs with more than 20 years' experience in the profession. A client-oriented Ace could be supported by testimonials from clients for whom the firm "went the extra mile" to solve a crisis.

THE STORY

Your core messages are used in developing the "story" about your business. This is not a company history, but rather a clearly defining story about what you stand for and how you positively affect your customers and your community.

Ideally, your story will appeal to the media, too. When your story is "bigger" than your company, and when it shows how you serve society at large or at least a large community, the media will be attracted to it.

The story should include your company's mission and your vision of where it is headed. The story can include a brief reference to your founding and your growth, but only if that directly links to how your strengths have enabled you to grow. The story should explain the qualifications of your firm and its staff members for the services it provides and/or the products it produces. Finally, the story should highlight your commitment to continuing on the same path of providing superior products and services in the future.

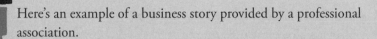

Here's an example of a business story provided by a professional association.

Since 1983, the National Association of Personal Financial Advisors (NAPFA) has offered individuals and families access to truly comprehensive, strictly fee-only financial advisors. NAPFA-registered financial advisors are committed to three principles: accepting no commissions or indirect payments for financial recommendations; providing comprehensive financial planning; and achieving the highest levels of competency.

NAPFA firmly believes that consumers of all income and wealth levels are entitled to objective, high-quality financial advice. For the most important financial decisions of their lives, people need advisors they can trust, who are working in their interests at all times.

NAPFA-registered financial advisors are compensated strictly on a fee-only basis. This means they do not accept commissions or any additional fees from outside sources for the recommendations they make. This aligns their interests solely with their clients. All NAPFA members make the additional public commitment of signing the organization's Fiduciary Oath, ensuring that they uphold the highest standards of integrity.

ELEVATOR STATEMENT

An elevator statement is a quick teaser about your business. In two or three sentences, you should be able to summarize the core message and state your Aces. The elevator statement should provoke a positive response from the listener, and strike his curiosity. Your goal is to generate an opportunity to go into further detail at an appropriate time.

The elevator statement is a distillation of the story of the firm. It focuses on what you do, and who you do it for. Consider the

NAPFA-registered financial advisors practice truly comprehensive financial planning, carefully integrating information on a wide range of typical consumer concerns. Financial services might include investments, taxes, estate plans, charitable giving, inheritance, health insurance, disability insurance, long-term care, business transitions, pensions and much more.

Through a rigorous application process and peer review, NAPFA members demonstrate that they can analyze an individual's entire financial situation and identify strategies for clients to successfully achieve all of life's milestones. A NAPFA-registered financial advisor's competence is assured through the expert review of a sample comprehensive financial plan, as well as proof of advanced training, three years of planning experience and ongoing education.

Ongoing turbulence in our economy has forced individuals and families to make tough financial decisions. More than ever, individuals and families need to be able to trust the professionals who they turn to for advice. NAPFA-registered financial advisors represent the highest standards of fiduciary conduct, comprehensive knowledge, and required training and experience.

several paragraphs of the "story" of the National Association of Personal Financial Advisors (NAPFA) above:

Consumers across the country look to The National Association of Personal Financial Advisors (NAPFA) for access to truly comprehensive, strictly fee-only financial advisors who meet the highest membership standards possible for fee-only compensation, professional competency and comprehensive financial planning, so you can achieve your financial dreams.

Whereas the story provided a great deal of detail on the core principles by which members of NAPFA operate and the strict qualifications for becoming a member, the elevator statement goes right to the heart of the matter: What does a NAPFA member do that others might not? With curiosity aroused by the elevator statement, a member of NAPFA would then have the opportunity to explain in greater detail what he or she does that is different from other financial services professionals.

TAGLINE

The tagline is the elevator statement reduced even further. The tagline is most likely to be (along with your name and logo) the first thing a person sees about your firm. It will be printed on all materials and shown prominently on your web site and heard in radio or television advertising.

Taglines must be only a few words and really cut to the point.

You have already seen how NAPFA's story was reduced to an elevator statement. Here now is that statement reduced to a tagline:

NAPFA: *Truly Comprehensive, Strictly Fee-Only*

Image

Tennis star Andre Agassi popularized the phrase "Image is everything." While it is not literally true—image is not "everything"—there's no doubt that image is critical to a company's, organization's and even a country's success.

Think about the most famous images in America: the flag; the Statue of Liberty; the U.S. Capitol Dome. These images elicit powerful, emotional responses.

The most successful companies in the world have developed images that are equally powerful in their own ways. The McDonald's arches, the classic Coke bottle or Mickey Mouse ears are indelibly etched in our minds. They bring about feelings of pleasure and nostalgia. They are known worldwide.

While it's unlikely that you can build an image that will have the same worldwide impact as McDonald's or *Coca-Cola*, you can develop an image that is deeply meaningful for a target audience.

Companies convey a great deal about themselves with their images. In the 1980s, Apple Computer's famous logo of a rainbow apple with a bite missing set the company apart from stodgy computer makers like IBM and Hewlett-Packard. Apple signaled that it was a rebel in the computer market, offering an easy-to-use computer for creative home users and small businesses. Apple was different from computer manufacturers that focused on expensive mainframes or stodgy number-crunching capabilities. Apple reinforced that image with its tagline, "Think Outside the Box."

By the way, an effective image does not have to be rebellious. Merrill Lynch's image is the venerable sign for stock market optimism, the bull. The image for Prudential Insurance is a mountain, as it promises you can "own a piece of the rock."

Images have been important to people for millennia. They have conveyed hope, fear, trust, power and every other human emotion.

Today, with the development of electronic media, the use of images has accelerated to an unprecedented degree. Images are everywhere, and they are bigger, bolder and brasher than ever, too.

Yet, a business's ability to place their images in front of people in multiplying rapidly, leading to the unfortunate effect of overwhelming consumers. People see too many images, and they have learned how to ignore many of them. It is up to you to find a way to break through the "noise."

As was indicated earlier, the Verbal Brand is the catalyst for creating just such an image. The companies we have been discussing have spent

A Michigan-based financial services firm with about 30 employees recently tried to strengthen its visual brand. Like a lot of firms in its market area, it was under the umbrella of a parent company, through which it sold personal and commercial lines of insurance. But the firm also had several sub-companies. One was a mortgage broker and another provided financial planning services. Because the firm proffered so many services (sound familiar?), its image suffered; it lacked a clear, united message that prospects could grab on to.

The first step was to change the firm's name, taking out the word "insurance" and replacing it with the more collective-sounding "group." Second, the web site was stripped of various logos that had represented each sub-company. The firm's business units were, in effect, competing with each other. The multiple logos were replaced with a single, uniform symbol. On the web site, each sub-company now rests under that one logo, but each is distinguished by having the sub-company name and logo in a different color.

hundreds of millions of dollars across decades of marketing to develop these messages. They know that the visual images represent what they are about. As the example above shows, even small companies can do the same thing, on a scale that is appropriate for them.

Reputation

Your reputation comes from everything you do. From how you work with clients and business partners. From how you treat employees. From how generous you are to your community. And from how accessible you are to the media.

Let's say that your area of expertise is advising other companies on how to create and manage employee 401(k) plans. Wouldn't you want a reputation as someone who clients refer friends and family to, and whom the media would call up for investment and retirement information?

When you write media pitches, you will do best initially by focusing on products and services that you have delivered in the past. Your reputation with news members will be much stronger when you can reference your accomplishments and satisfied customers. You can be sure that a reporter will ask to contact your clients and customers as a way to verify your performance, and also to expand the news report so that it has appeal to the media outlet's wide audience.

Developing a strong reputation based on your work with past customers is not enough, though. The other critical aspect is to prudently manage your media relationships. Even if you are respected by your customers, if you mishandle your press relations, your reputation will suffer. This does not represent media bias against your company; it's basic human nature. A reporter's impression of your firm is influenced by many factors, and one of the most important is how you interact with him or her. If you make statements that are exaggerated or untrue, or if you do not respond to a reporter's questions by the deadline promised, then your reputation will suffer, sometimes considerably.

Building a reputation is a long-term strategy, and it requires constant attention. A reputation can perhaps be given a short-term boost through a high-profile advertising campaign, but you will be disappointed by the long-term result. It is the equivalent of Kato Kaelin's 15 minutes of fame during the O.J. Simpson trial, and it will have about as much lasting value.

Conclusion: Success

When you create a strong Name, a memorable Verbal Brand Image, and a positive Reputation, your firm is poised for Success. That's $N+I+R=S_2$. Prospective customers and clients will understand instantly what your firm does better than anyone else.

Success with the media follows the same tried-and-true path. News producers want to learn about you, and they are eager to understand who you are and what expertise you can provide. Your pitch can give them a positive initial glimpse of you and your company. If you can prove your information will help them do their jobs better, they will contact you regularly and will reflect you positively in their articles.

Making the perfect pitch requires combining many elements, including perfect timing. You must have the right brand; develop the right name, image, and reputation; and find the right audience–with whom you've already built up a strong relationship. That's a tall challenge. But one that can be met by taking meaningful, manageable steps.

CHAPTER 3

The Foundation of Media Rapport

THE FOUNDATION OF *Media Rapport*

I n my years helping business owners build PR campaigns, I have stressed that PR and pitching are person-to-person activities. There is no substitute for having a professional relationship— rapport—with individual members of the media. This does not imply that you need to become a reporter's best friend. In fact, the best reporters maintain a distant relationship from even their most prized sources. But you do need to develop a working rapport that enables you to contact him or her and exchange ideas. When you have rapport, you will be able to truly explain how your products and services benefit the marketplace.

Rapport is another way of saying that the reporter trusts you, and will turn to you for analysis of complex issues and predictions about trends in your industry. Building rapport requires being able to offer the "unit of exchange" that means the most in the media: useful, reliable, and timely information. Then you will regularly be at the front of a reporter's e-mail contact list or Rolodex.

In this chapter, we discuss how to leverage your skills and knowledge in order to generate appealing and timely information. You'll also learn how to take the initial steps towards crafting the pitch and building the rapport that will ultimately deliver the attention you seek.

Building Blocks of Media Rapport

It's useful to think of media rapport as being represented by the four cornerstones of a building, with each encompassing a crucial element for creating the long-term, high-trust relationship with the media. The cornerstones of the foundation are your message, your skills/knowledge, respect and your pitch.

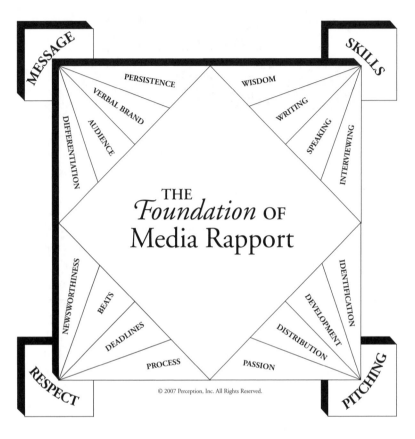

MESSAGE

SKILLS

PERSISTENCE
WISDOM
VERBAL BRAND
WRITING
DIFFERENTIATION
AUDIENCE
SPEAKING
INTERVIEWING

THE
Foundation OF
Media Rapport

NEWSWORTHINESS
IDENTIFICATION
BEATS
DEVELOPMENT
DEADLINES
DISTRIBUTION
RESPECT
PROCESS
PASSION
PITCHING

It's not an accident that I have placed the pitch as the fourth cornerstone. Pitching evolves from the solidity of the other three cornerstones. A good pitch begins with 1) a well-targeted message; 2) skills to present to the media; and 3) a positive media response because you've demonstrated respect for their needs. Then, the pitch will achieve results. Just as importantly, with those three cornerstones in place, the pitch serves to strengthen the foundation you laid.

Each foundation cornerstone consists of several building blocks.

MESSAGE

What is it about your profession or industry or company you want to share with consumers? What opportunities are available for your customers? How do you help customers and prospects take advantage of opportunities and avoid risks and emerging threats? These matters must come through loud and clear in your message.

Your message includes four building blocks:

- *Verbal Brand.* You have already developed your Verbal Brand through the exercises in Chapter 2. Keep your Verbal Brand in mind at all times as you develop your message to the media. Make sure that the message reflects and supports the Verbal Brand. This unique message is what differentiates you from your competitors, who also seek the same airtime and print space.

- *Audience.* Who is the audience for your message? Be as specific as possible, using some of the knowledge you gained from your branding work.

  Defining an audience is more difficult than it may appear initially because your pitching message has three of them. First, you have your customers and clients who already work with you and (hopefully) feel good about your services. You can use your message to strengthen ties with your current customer base.

  Second, you have your audience of potential customers, as defined in your Verbal Brand exercises. This is a much larger group than your current customer base, and it may include different subgroups that are seeking different products or services. When crafting your message, you need to think about which target audience groups to reach. You must select a group with enough shared interests that a single message in your pitch will be meaningful to them, while recognizing that a single pitch cannot appeal to all possible customers.

  Third, you have the audience that reads the publication or watches or listens to the show to which you are pitching. Your message must be appropriate for this group, even if it's not of primary importance to the entire audience. No matter how great your pitch, if it's not relevant for a publication's readers or a show's

There are several ways to build a message. Consider:

Using Anecdotes

Anecdotes and stories are among the most effective ways to develop a message. A story grabs the reader's interest by personalizing an abstract issue, enabling the reader to put himself in someone else's shoes. The telling of the story brings out the technical expertise needed to solve the problem—the expertise that you provide.

Consumer finance publications make prominent use of these stories in their columns and feature articles by introducing a family with a financial problem, which is then solved by expert financial advisors. So if you were to pitch an article to a consumer finance publication, you might suggest a client with a money problem that's interesting to its readers (and offer yourself as one of the experts to analyze the problem).

Local Color

If your business is highly localized, such as a restaurant, bringing local color into a pitch is often effective. Local TV newscasts favor this approach, for example. Their reporters take a general topic—such as the problems with high-carbohydrate foods offered at fast food restaurants—and they localize it by filming in front of a particular fast food restaurant in the region. Localization provides the viewer with a sense that he is potentially affected by the issue—*Hey, I've been to that restaurant!*—and so he continues

viewers, it will not be used. You must find the sweet spot in which you can reach both your target audiences—and develop a message that speaks to this unique group.

to watch the report. If your business serves a local audience, it's easy for you to make sure that your pitch carries this "local flavor."

Variation on a Theme

Let's say you have a business that advises parents on paying for their children's education and you also have various investment products to help them achieve their savings goals. Your general message would be about the high cost of a college education, but you could develop six separate pitches that each provides a different savings or investment strategy. By distributing these pitches on a monthly basis, you are much more likely to reach a reporter at the right time, with the right idea.

A Regular Report

Some relationships evolve over years on the basis of a regular report that an expert releases regularly to the media. Reporters begin to rely on them for historical industry trends and look forward to the report as a source of ideas each week or month. One of the most successful examples is the Lundberg Survey, a nationwide survey of average retail gasoline prices across the United States. First developed by Jack Lundberg in the 1950s for oil industry clients, the consumer-friendly Lundberg Survey debuted in 1973. This is a weekly summary of gasoline prices on a national and regional basis distributed to the mass media. The Lundberg Survey is cited in countless newspaper and web articles and TV and radio reports each year, and Jack's daughter Trilby has parlayed the popularity of the report into hundreds of media appearances and a thriving energy consulting business.

- *Differentiation.* It's critical you differentiate your message from others the media receives. Referencing your Verbal Brand will help with differentiation, but it's not enough. Your pitch should provide information that is new. Perhaps it's a new solution to an old problem, or the emergence of a new problem, or a new or improved product.

- *Persistence.* Members of the media receive many news releases and pitches from many sources. Even a perfectly targeted and well-conceived pitch is often lost in the flood of information a reporter receives. For this reason, you must be persistent, and even relentless, in sharing your ideas.

One e-mail pitch to a favorite reporter is not enough. You must come up with a series of ideas, all related to the same theme, and send them on a consistent basis. Each idea should reinforce the same basic message (and your Verbal Brand), but should have enough detail so that it might be the one to generate a response.

SKILLS

A message is most effective when it's supported by a person who has superior communications skills. If you cannot explain your idea and provide real-life examples, your media contacts will likely lose interest. Remember that communicating is their lifeblood, and they need to work with people who can express ideas and provide facts and analysis in an entertaining way.

Be assured reporters understand that you might not be a polished speaker, nor ready with a quip like a stand-up comic. They do expect you to be able to explain your ideas in easily digestible terms, without a great deal of industry jargon.

Your interaction with the media will likely come in several forms over the years, including your written pitches, phone and in-person interviews and public speaking engagements. As you think about your long-term PR plans, you should enhance your skills in each of these areas.

- *Writing.* Even in our era of cable television news and iPod downloads, the written word is at the heart of our Information Age media. People have their favorite publications—on paper or online—for news, finance, sports, entertainment and so on. They go to these sources perhaps more than ever, because they are so easily accessed day and night. Your pitch will be successful if you communicate clear information that is easily transformed into the written articles you already see produced.

You might not be a superb writer and be tempted to hire a staffer or freelancer to do all your writing. However, in my experience working with clients in many professions, I have found that all of them benefit from making an effort to put their ideas into sentences and paragraphs. Business owners and executives might not have the time to complete a perfect draft of an article or a pitch, but the discipline involved in writing the first draft usually contributes to a more complete presentation.

When writing to, or for, a member of the media, keep in mind the tight deadlines they face. Too often, people want to ensure the story idea they are sharing is explained in enough detail so the reporter knows exactly what they mean. However, that level of detail often is overkill.

We all have heard about the K.I.S.S. principle: Keep It Simple, Stupid. This applies to working with the media. Journalists did not get to where they are because they are fools. They are intelligent people who can determine a potential story's value within seconds – and seconds is often all the time they have to consider your pitch! As you will learn in Chapter 5, your pitch should get to the point quickly. Your key assertion should be upfront. The assertion should be supported with facts (especially statistics and data) to back up your claim. Then you quickly close your pitch with your contact information. That's it. If the reporter wants more information, he or she will contact you.

- *Interviewing.* If your pitch is effective, it will generate a response, often in the form of a telephone interview. Usually, you do not have time to prepare in advance for the conversation. So you must work on your interview skills while you are making your pitch, and be prepared for a call at any time.

Perfecting The Pitch by Benjamin Lewis

Responding to interview questions is an art and a science, and entire books have been written on the subject. But here are a few simple rules that can help you:

- Practice your answers to questions you anticipate.
- Respond to questions you receive.
- Keep your answers short.
- If there is something you especially want to emphasize, then say it. Tell the reporter, "This is very important...."
- Speak slowly and clearly.
- Make sure you can document any assertions you make.
- Do not use humor unless it's very obvious and harmless. Humor taken out of context always causes trouble.

Improving Your Communications Skills

Many business leaders who are not good writers or who do not have good speaking skills would prefer to outsource those tasks to others. While this may be more efficient in the short-term, it's not a good strategy over time. You are your most effective spokesperson, and eventually, you will need to write and speak on behalf of your organization.

The first thing you need to do is to recognize your weaknesses, preferably by showing your writing samples to a few good writers. Ask them for honest feedback. Find out if you are using too much jargon, or if you are being too informal.

If your concern is public speaking, then ask for feedback from people who have heard you speak. Almost every conference organizer distributes speaker evaluation forms. Ask for your evaluation, both your numeric score and attendee comments.

Once you've learned about your strengths and weaknesses, work on the areas that need improvement. Numerous workshops and dozens of books are available to help business executives "master the art" of business writing or public speaking.

- Avoid making negative remarks unless they are directly relevant and backed up with firm facts.
- Do not assume that your comments are "off the record," even if you said they are. Operate on the assumption that everything is fair game.

- *Speaking.* Public speaking energizes some people, and it fills others with anxiety. Yet, to represent your company effectively to the public (not just the media), you need to be able to articulate your Verbal Brand and more. Remember that you are in the best position to describe your company and its qualifications because you know the company better than anyone else.

You also need to commit yourself to regular practice. Write for your company's newsletter, web site or blog; contribute to industry journals (even if it's only a letter to the editor); and work on your pitches, of course. Seek out opportunities to speak at conferences or online seminars. Consider joining a Toastmasters group in your area. Within a short time, you will enjoy significant improvement.

Here are some publications and organizations that provide excellent training and ideas for writing and speaking:

Zig Ziglar's personal development Web site – www.ZiglarOnline.com

Toastmasters International – www.Toastmasters.org

Dale Carnegie Training – www.DaleCarnegie.com

Leaders Institute – www.LeadersInstitute.com

Public Relations Society of America – www.PRSA.org

League of American Communications Professionals – www.LACP.com

Chicago Manual of Style – www.ChicagoManualofStyle.com

The Associated Press Stylebook – www.APStyleBook.com

When it comes to speaking, practice makes perfect. I speak at
financial industry conferences and events around the country,
and there has not been a time when I didn't get a little nervous or
anxious. Nervousness can be overcome. It comes from knowing
the material and having confidence in yourself and your message.

When speaking with reporters, you need to be confident. If you
lack confidence in what you're saying, they will hear it, see it and
sense it. They will begin to doubt whether you know what you're
talking about, and whether you are a reliable resource. Passion is
also important (as you already learned earlier in the book). Being
confident and having passion can be a terrific combination, even
with the most cynical member of the media.

- *Wisdom.* Wisdom is the glue that holds your skills cornerstone
together. You demonstrate your wisdom through your writing
and speaking—but only if you have developed that knowledge
in the first place. Do not oversell your familiarity with a subject,
nor your past performance; stick with what you can do and have
done. Gradually, you will become more wise and polished and can
expand your pitching accordingly.

RESPECT

It's not easy to be a reporter or an editor. Deadline pressures are
immense, and they are getting tougher, due to the caliber and
number of instant news services on the Web. Reporters are usually
jugging multiple articles, with varying deadlines, while also trying
to stay abreast of new developments so that they can start their
research for future articles.

More than the multiple deadlines, reporters and editors face intense
pressures for accuracy. Think about what happens when you make
a mistake in a memo to a client or a price quote to a prospect. You
see the mistake, and you correct it, or the client sees the mistake
and asks you to clarify. It's a private matter among a relatively small
number of people. Now think about what happens when a member
of the media makes a mistake: It's out there for all to see. Especially

today, with the advent of blogs, every article and news telecast is open to immediate, and often vicious, public comment. By its very nature, the news business is a public venture in ways that are unimaginable in almost any other industry or profession.

Therefore, journalists must learn to balance their deadlines ("the need for speed") with getting the facts right. This means that they have to find sources who respect their needs for timeliness, accuracy, objectivity and completeness. If you can deliver on those measures, you will go a long way towards building rapport with the media.

A reporter's life can be seen through the prism of beats, newsworthiness, process and deadlines. Understanding these aspects will help you work with the media in ways that generate mutual respect.

Beat. A "beat" is the term used to describe a primary area of coverage for a reporter. A local newspaper reporter might have the city council as a beat. A *Wall Street Journal* reporter might have Microsoft as a beat. Most reporters have multiple, overlapping beats.

A reporter is responsible for staying on top of all the news in his or her beat, as well as generating news stories and ideas for more extensive feature articles from that beat. A reporter is often graded by whether competing publications have "scooped" him with an important story. A reporter who is scooped too many times does not have a job.

In thinking about which reporters you wish to contact with your pitch, you should be aware of beats. Surely there is a reporter at each publication you target who has a beat that is naturally related to your pitch topic. You can figure out who it is by looking at who wrote the articles covering topics relevant to you business. Most likely, that person should be your first contact point at the publication.

While thinking about a reporter's beat, determine if the reporting is balanced with comments from both sides of an issue. Does the reporter stick to the facts, or look for the human-interest angle? Does the reporter seem to know a lot about your industry, or is he/she apparently still low on the learning curve? Is the reporter usually critical of a specific service or product?

For example, if a reporter who covers the automotive industry typically criticizes American automakers, it does not make sense to encourage this reporter to write about the features of new Chrysler LeBarons at your car dealership. That reporter should be lower on your priority list than another reporter. If you choose to seek the attention of the reporter who apparently dislikes American-made cars, your pitch should acknowledge the flaws with Chrysler automobiles that the reporter has noted in the past, but which this LeBaron has addressed.

Here's a tip: Before pitching a reporter, go to Google.com. Type in the reporter's name and search for him or her under the "News" option. Read recent articles with their byline. Incorporate what you learn about the reporter's beat, style and interests into your pitch. This simple effort can significantly increase your chances of gaining placement.

- *Newsworthiness.* Within a beat, a reporter must make judgments about which articles are most valuable or newsworthy. Obviously the reporter cannot cover everything every day. There simply isn't time to produce all the information (in print, radio or TV), and there isn't anywhere to publish it even if it could be produced. The Web has changed this dynamic slightly, as it has few inherent limitations on how much information can be provided; but a reporter and editor still must make a judgment about which information is most valuable (newsworthy) and deserving of primary locations on a site.

In thinking about your pitch, put yourself in a reporter's shoes. Make your idea as newsworthy as possible. Does it affect people now, or in the near future? If the answer's now, it's likely to be more newsworthy. Does it affect a significant number of people? Is the effect large? Again, an issue that affects more people is more newsworthy. Can the issue be explained fairly easily (reporters avoid stories that require readers to have a Ph.D. in biochemistry)? The more strongly you can answer "yes" to these questions, the more newsworthy your pitch will be.

If you can support your pitch with specific solutions, then you have an even stronger pitch.

Process. Each media organization has a different process for its news cycle, and it's not likely that you will be able to find this out until you have a working relationship with a reporter or editor. Yet, it's helpful to understand the general operations of most media outlets, even as you are initiating your PR and pitching program.

Typically, a reporter suggests an idea to an editor, and then the editor either says yes or no or suggests a modified idea. Sometimes, an editor suggests an idea and assigns it to a reporter, but usually, the reporter is the "eyes and ears" of the media organization, and his or her suggestions carry great weight. Thus, you want to approach the reporter with your pitch—not the editor.

Also, publications have reporting cycles tied to how often they publish. A monthly magazine has monthly deadlines; a daily newspaper has daily deadlines; a web site might have hourly deadlines. Be sensitive to deadlines the reporter is facing, and make sure to time your pitch appropriately.

Timing is crucial. You must make your pitch far enough in advance of publication that the reporter will have time to research the story and complete it by the deadline; otherwise it's not newsworthy. For example, if you are a developer showing an energy-efficient model home, you need to inform monthly publications at least three months in advance. That monthly reporter is probably working in February on articles that will appear in the May issue (when your open house will take place); this is especially common for publications that use a great deal of photography; articles and photos are prepared well in advance. However, you could pitch the same story to your local daily newspaper two weeks in advance, because that reporter is probably juggling a half-dozen stories due over a shorter period of time. The daily newspaper has not yet focused on an event that is two weeks away.

The third critical issue is understanding that, in many instances, the reporter will not rely on you as the sole source for an article, even if you presented the original idea. Reporters are trained to speak with many people—especially people who have different perspectives on the issue—so that a balanced view can be presented. You need to be prepared for a reporter to call your competitors, or people who disagree with you, and to have those viewpoints in the same article. The reporter might even call you a second or third time and ask tougher questions if other people raised issues that were not discussed initially. This is where your interview skills are important, because you have to be ready to discuss difficult, and even unpleasant, matters the reporter has raised.

- *Deadlines.* Reporters live and die by deadlines. If you wish to develop a strong rapport with a reporter, you need to respect the deadlines that he faces. There is no single issue that is more important to building your relationship than respecting those deadlines.

Respect for deadlines comes into effect in several ways. When a reporter gives you a deadline to respond to his questions, that deadline is real. It's not an approximate date or time; it's a real deadline. Think about the deadlines that your firm faces—whether it's submitting a contract proposal, filing a court document, or collecting rent. Now multiply that occurrence by several sources for each story, and several stories (or more) each week. Now you can start to get a sense of how a reporter operates. Furthermore, this reporter is feeding news into an organization with multiple reporters and editors, which raises the complexity of the publication's deadline even further.

So when a reporter states a deadline, you need to be very confident that you can meet that deadline with your response. If you cannot meet the deadline, then be honest. Ask for a later deadline. Ask if a compromise can be arranged. Maybe you can provide some information that the reporter is seeking by email, but just not all of it. Maybe the reporter is doing a follow-up story the next week, and you can provide information for that story. Maybe the reporter does have some deadline flexibility and can give you another day to respond. Bottom line: Make sure that if you agree to a deadline, you meet your obligation.

Respecting deadlines also comes into effect when you contact a reporter with your pitch. Be aware that the reporter might be on a deadline for another article or another publication. The reporter may not be able to speak with you at that time, nor even to respond to an email note. The reporter might not be able to focus on your pitch for a few days or even a few weeks—simply because other deadlines have a greater priority. This is why short, concise pitches sent regularly are the best way to work with reporters. Short pitches minimize the time demands on the reporters while keeping you near the forefront of their minds as a possible source of valuable information.

PITCHING

The final cornerstone of building rapport with the media is the art of pitching your ideas. Later in this book, I will show you how to develop a pitch and list in detail specific "do's and don'ts" about pitching that have been identified by working reporters in an exclusive survey. Right now, I will focus on the general elements of the pitch: development, identification, distribution, and passion.

- *Development.* As we have seen, the creation of a pitch begins well in advance of actually writing and distributing an idea to the media. It begins by understanding your company, developing your Verbal Brand and targeting your pitch to appeal to both a specific type of customer and the audience of a specific media outlet. The pitch also must be well-written, concise and newsworthy.

None of these aspects is especially difficult to master if you are writing or talking about a subject that you know well and care about. The key is to pay attention to all of these elements. Developing your pitch is part of an ongoing process of thinking about your skills, your market, and where you want to be headed. It's not merely putting down on paper or in an e-mail the first idea that comes to mind.

- *Identification.* Previous exercises have emphasized that a successful pitch has a well-targeted audience that identifies with your ideas, products and solutions. As you generate a series of media contacts, they will start to identify you with certain skills and market expertise. These will be your prime opportunities for comments and analysis.

- *Distribution.* Deciding where, when and how you are distributing your pitch is integral to its success. Start with the publications and electronic media you find most valuable and pertinent to your own business. If you are reading certain publications, it's a good guess that your clients and prospects are, too. You can also ask your clients and customers where they go for information, and which resources they consider most trustworthy.

With the "where" decided initially, the "when" and "how" questions become fairly easy to determine. You can quickly figure out the deadline cycles of the media outlets that you are contacting, and you should set your frequency of pitches to match. Often, you can find out more information by making a quick phone call to a reporter who you have targeted and ask two simple questions: What is a good time to send you story pitches? In which format would you like them (email, fax, phone)?

Going Above And Beyond

To truly develop a long-lasting, positive relationship with the media, you must be prepared to do more than simply send information and fulfill media requests. If you can go "above and beyond" the call of duty, you will cement your credibility.

Journalists are excellent communicators. They can quickly absorb new facts and understand new situations. But this does not mean that they are experts in your industry. An automotive sector reporter, for example, can give his audience a description of how a car handles and which features are most attractive. Yet, that reporter may not know how, or why, those new features operate as they do. A financial journalist for a national newspaper can write about the latest investment trends and investment products, but she is not working with real clients making the investments. You're in a special position to explain in detail how things work, and to show reporters the practical, real-world applications of technologies, products and services.

Going "above and beyond" means making the extra effort to help the reporter understand that linkage. If you come across a statistic or a new study, share it. If you have a client or customer who is willing to be a real-life source, tell the reporter. If a reporter calls to bounce a couple of ideas off you because you are the expert, be helpful. Each of these will solidify the Foundation of Media Rapport.

How does going "above and beyond" help you? Here's how:

1. **Relationship Building** – You want to be viewed as a resource willing to do what it takes to make the reporter's job easier. A happy journalist will keep coming back.

2. **Word of Mouth** – Colleagues at newspapers or TV stations share sources and read competitors' articles or newscasts. If you have developed a reputation as a good source, you will get more calls and e-mails for interviews. Rather than having one great contact at only one outlet, you may end up with three, four, or more. Think of it as the equivalent of having a client who becomes your advocate and refers you to his friends. The better you can do for your media "clients," the more business it will mean for you.

Tip/Idea

We are strong believers that members of the media need to be recognized for a job well done. Reporters appreciate knowing that people are reading what they are reporting on (or watching their reports). We encourage all of our clients to send "Thank You" notes to journalists from time to time, referencing a specific article or observation that they found to be valuable.

A handwritten note is a powerful tool in your rapport-building arsenal. It shows you are paying attention, it shows you care, and it keeps your name front and center.

First is a note you might sent to a reporter who did not speak to you, but who covered a topic related to your business:

Dear Steve,

I just wanted to take a moment to thank you for writing the story on the growing problem of leaking underground storage tanks. The problem is more serious and more widespread than most people realize. My company has been working with large chemical developers

3. **Friendships** – Ultimately, you want to be viewed similarly to a friend by the media. A friend won't steer you wrong, won't take advantage of you and will always be there when needed. Going "above and beyond" not only creates a working relationship, but this type of "friendship." The first time you can pick up the phone and just have a conversation with a member of the media, whether it's about the weather, family or some other non-related industry topic, you know you will have created a friendship.

4. **Business Opportunities** – Reporters know people. In fact, they know many people. If they are impressed with you, your company

to advance clean-up procedures for several years. If we can help you in the future, please do not hesitate to call on us.

Thanks again,
Roger Sanders
Environmental Clean-Up, Inc.

Here is a thank-you note that you might send to a reporter who interviewed you for an article:

Dear Melinda,

Thank you for the opportunity today to let me share my observations about the growing need for 401(k) advice services in top corporations. This is a really important issue for all the retiring baby boomers who don't have pensions to protect them. Your work will help people understand the options they have a little better.

If I can be of assistance to you in the future, please let me know. I will make myself available to you whenever you need a resource on this important issue.

Warm Regards,
Betty Jones
401(k) Advisory Services, LLC.

and your product or service, they will recommend you to others. We hear members of the media tell us stories about how they use a financial advisor because they had a good experience on past stories. Some even recommended specific financial advisors to their family, friends and audience members based on those past conversations. The same story applies to any other service industry.

Going "above and beyond" should never be forgotten. Professionals, business owners, experts and others who just do the minimum will fade into obscurity. Doing everything you can to help them do their jobs a little bit better will keep you top of mind.

CHAPTER 4

Pitching

S o far, we have discussed the importance of pitching, and placed it in the context of your branding and marketing activities. This chapter focuses on what defines a pitch and how pitching it differs from other forms of media contact, such as press releases or paid advertising.

The benefits of a pitch can far exceed those of a press release or paid advertising, and for a fraction of the cost if done correctly. Yet, the principles of pitching are quite similar to traditional advertising and marketing practices. Just like advertising, pitching requires understanding your company and its markets, as well as being familiar with the media reaching your targeted customer base. Without knowing which news outlets you are seeking (and which staff members of those outlets), you will struggle to reach the right audience.

In understanding how to create and distribute your pitch, you also need to understand what pitching is not. Pitching is not sending out mass mailings of media releases to every contact name you purchased in a directory. Pitching is not sending an email to editors in order to announce that you just hired a new executive. Pitching is not advertising, nor is it paid promotion.

Pitching: What It Is

Pitching can be defined as developing targeted messages that highlight the unique attributes of your company or organization to specific media outlets. In other words, the focus is on the message and not the medium.

Let's consider each element with the definition of a pitch:

- targeted messages;

- unique attributes; and

- specific media outlets.

Targeted messages. Having targeted messages is critical, and that is why I devoted Chapter 2 to the procedure for identifying your company's unique strengths.

A pitch consists of a single message or topic that directly relates to one of your operational strengths. Often, the pitch is timely.

Unique Attributes. The best pitches focus on specific attributes and features that a company or organization offers. It is that uniqueness that often grabs a reporter's attention and places your pitch above a more generic competitor's.

An Example of a Timely Pitch

Identity theft of financial data is a major consumer concern today. Banks, credit card companies, mortgage lenders and other financial institutions are now reporting an increased number of security breaches that put customers' private financial information at risk. Many states now require public announcements of major breaches, and so these incidents have become regular news items. In addition to news reports, news outlets often offer advice about how the typical consumer can protect against these threats and fraud.

A bank vice president at Main Street Bank sees the media's need for accurate information on security breaches as an opportunity for a pitch. Main Street Bank works hard to assure current and potential customers that it is protecting their assets. The bank wants to get this message to the public in as many ways as possible. However, it doesn't do much good for Main Street Bank to send out a press release that says, "We have great online security." Every bank makes this claim.

The National Association of Personal Financial Advisors (NAPFA) provides a good illustration of how to define unique attributes and use them in pitches. NAPFA, first introduced in the last chapter, is a trade association of "fee-only," comprehensive financial advisors in North America. NAPFA members embrace a unique set of principles considered more stringent and consumer-friendly than some other financial advisors. When NAPFA members say they are "fee only," this means that they do not accept any forms of commissions, fee, or discounts from the providers of financial services. Their entire compensation comes directly from their clients. This principle stands in contrast to

Instead, the bank might send a pitch about its particular state-of-the-art online security technology. With that message, news agencies have something specific to report. The pitch will need to include specific information, briefly, about both the problem and the bank's solution. Just a few paragraphs to whet a reporter's appetite, so that the bank will receive a media inquiry for an interview.

When the call comes for the interview, the bank will be able to present a wide range of information about its security procedures. The vice president who initiated the pitch can talk about the bank's policy and the importance it places on security. The bank's security representative can talk about the new technology, and she can also suggest follow-up interviews with other bank staff and officers who have security responsibility. The bank will become a resource for security information, in the mind of the reporter.

However, the bank also must be prepared to back up its claim that it is operating with state-of-the-art standards, or its message will fall flat. As discussed in Chapter 3, the bank will damage its reputation if it makes a claim that it cannot live up to. Its rapport with the media might be permanently damaged.

more than 95 percent of financial advisors in North America, who rely completely or primarily on commissions to earn their livings.

NAPFA members are truly different, and this is easily identified by their fee-only compensation status. When NAPFA is seeking to attract media attention, it selects opportunities that enable it to highlight the importance of using a fee-only financial advisor. The opportunity might be a new study that indicates consumers' preferences for advisors who do not accept commissions. Or a new law related to how advisors must disclose the commissions they receive. Or a new questionnaire, created by a consumer-rights organization, to help individuals understand how their advisor is being compensated. With each example, NAPFA can maneuver its members' unique compensation into its pitch.

Just as importantly, NAPFA does not create media pitches that focus on issues where its membership is not differentiated from the mass of financial advisors. For example, NAPFA does not produce media pitches about investment returns, even though most NAPFA members are federally-approved Registered Investment Advisors. NAPFA does not produce media pitches about taxes, even though many of its members are CPAs who provide sophisticated tax advice. These are not the unique attributes in the financial advisor arena.

Specific Media Outlets. Selecting the correct media outlets is as important as having a good message. You must consider all media relevant to a target audience and tailor your message appropriately for each. The pitch will have to appeal to the interests of a publication's readers or television program's viewers, and it will have to be on the right sophistication level, too. Also, the pitch will have to draw attention to your organization's capabilities, while not coming across like a direct sales effort.

Consider a company that provides environmental services to clean up leaking fuel tanks at gasoline stations. The company would begin by targeting publications read by gas station owners, who likely are highly interested in legal updates regarding storage tanks, the ways to identify leaks and cost-effective cleanup solutions. Pitches to the reporters and editors of these publications would focus on the company's technically trained experts, and the pitches would use terminology such as "remediation," which is the industry's term for cleanup. Data might be included in the pitch, such as the average costs and time spent on remediation, as well as technology options that the company can provide.

On the other hand, the same company might wish to expand into new lines of business in environmental services. To support this effort, it might develop a different series of news pitches targeting broader publications that include environmental services. Again, the company would cite its expertise in one particular area, but a pitch would also reference the needs of the entire remediation industry, including hazardous waste sites, nuclear waste sites, munitions dumps, etc. Rather than providing specific information about fuel storage tank remediation, a pitch might instead show how expertise in storage tanks can transfer to other types of remediation activities.

Yet even as this remediation company seeks to build its name recognition, pitching to consumer-oriented environmental publications is probably outside of its domain. At first, it might seem as if environmental magazines are an appropriate audience, because the company is providing solutions that clean the environment. However, mass-market environmental magazines likely lack savvy readers that can digest too many technical details about storage tank cleanup. Only a small fraction of readers are likely to be buyers of the company's services—and those readers are likely to be professionals who already read the trade journals.

Even if consumer publications are not a good target for a pitch, this same fuel storage tank remediation company still might have opportunities to reach out to a broader audience. Let's consider what the company can do if it has a proven cleanup method, and it wants to earn recognition from the business community at large in order to support ambitious growth plans. Consumer-oriented environmental publications are not appropriate. Instead, the company could target general business publications, some of which reach more than one million readers per issue. The firm would focus its story pitches on why its training programs have generated extraordinary customer satisfaction ratings; or that it is the first company in its industry to offer franchises; or how it adapted a technology originally developed by the pharmaceutical industry to the fuel storage tank problem. Through these types of pitches, the company can extend recognition outside of its industry, and then leverage its coverage when it is seeking a large bank loan for expansion or trying to sell franchise opportunities.

It should be noted that pitching to mass-circulation publications is not always a poor idea. Far from it. When a company is providing a product or service directly to consumers, it is hugely beneficial to get recognition in a national consumer publication, network television show, major cable program or a widely read web site. The mass media can act as rocket fuel for growth because of their influence. But reaching these is also the trickiest, most challenging type of pitch, and the one that takes the longest to develop. For those pitches, extra patience must be exercised.

Four Criteria of News

Regardless of the media outlet, a pitch must contain newsworthy information or it will quickly be deleted from an email account or thrown in the trash can.

While judging what is news can be as much an art as a science, journalists are trained to seek ideas that will capture their readers' interests and are relevant to their readers' lives. Journalists hone this sense during their tenure at various publications, and they develop a feel for both the subject matter and the treatment of that subject that will hold the interest of their audience.

Your pitch will be more successful if it helps a journalist begin to take those steps towards a newsworthy story. While a good journalist can probably make a story out of almost anything (and sometimes critics accuse journalists of doing just that!), the truth is that journalists are so busy that often they do not have the time to reflect carefully upon how to bring out the best news value in an idea. If your pitch is well-designed, it will point the recipient towards that idea.

Here are four primary attributes that journalists are seeking when they make their rapid-fire judgment about whether your pitch is newsworthy:

- *Is the idea timely?* Timeliness is perhaps the single-most important factor in determining whether an idea or an article is pursued. Editors are in a constant race against their competition. A story that is timely—within the deadline parameters of the publica- tion—will always attract the greatest attention.

  This means you must look at current issues to see what's already been covered. As a professional in your field, you are in an ideal position to think about the trends. In fact, you are surely doing this anyway as part of your business activities and strategizing. Think about how you can share some of those ideas with the media.

  Again, make sure that you are sharing the right idea with the right publication. For a business-to-business publication that covers government regulation, you could pitch a story about a new law that is coming in a few months, but which you are already in compliance. Showing that you are ahead of the curve would defi- nitely be an interesting pitch.

- *Is the idea unusual?* Obviously, it's difficult for every idea to be unique or even unusual. But you should be especially attentive to when you have the opportunity to communicate a new idea, procedure or product that only you provide. Journalists are always on the lookout for companies or individuals who are doing some- thing unusual, especially if it has the potential for wider adoption in the future.

One example later in this book references a financial advisory firm that developed its own brand of mutual fund, based on the investing principles devised (and proven to be effective) by its owners. The branded mutual fund enabled investors who were not clients of the firm to benefit from the financial expertise that the firm had developed over the previous 20 years. This pitch had appeal to numerous mass-market and specialty investment publications.

Ideas tied to entertainment also may attract journalists because they promise a departure from the usual fare of news stories. This is why many publications include articles about celebrities, charity events or features about interesting individuals. When you are able to link your idea to something with entertainment value, it stands a better chance of being selected from the pack.

This does not mean that, if you own a car dealership, you need to hire socialite Paris Hilton for a grand opening celebration (although that probably would attract media attention). You can do something much simpler and less costly, such as providing free use of cars for golfers when they come to your city for an annual PGA Tour event. Write a pitch about which cars you're providing golfers and why they like them. You don't even have to wait for a special event, if you think about the in-house "stories" among your staff. For example, one of the guys in your service center is a promising stock car racer on the weekends. Your sponsorship of his car would be a very appealing feature pitch.

- *Is the idea controversial?* Your industry probably has its share of controversies. Maybe they relate to regulations or a high-profile lawsuit; maybe they related to a technological innovation; or maybe they related to new forms of competition hitting the marketplace. Regardless of the source of controversy, the media covering your industry are covering the controversy, too.

You need to define your position on the controversial issue of the day. Develop a pitch that explains your position. Make sure you can back up your side of the argument with facts, as well as opinion.

➤ *Is the idea relevant to the majority of the audience?* Journalists recognize that they are writing for multiple, overlapping audiences. It's impossible for every article in a publication to appeal to every reader. But the publication must contain a range of articles that entice a large share of its readership base, or the readers will leave. So in weighing which articles to write (and whether to give them primary or secondary attention), journalists and editors favor articles relevant to the greatest number of readers.

You can do the same thing. If possible, include in your pitch a reference to the type and/or number of people affected by your idea for a story. This will help signal to a journalist that the idea will be meaningful to her readers.

For example, if you are a tax expert and you wish to pitch an article about how a new law will create new tax-savings opportunities, you could include a reference to the types of people impacted by the legislation. Even if you do not have a firm number, give a description of the types of people, so the journalist can consider the pitch in context.

Consider this comparison. Weak pitch: "A new federal tax law coming into effect this year will increase the deduction for equipment purchases for small businesses from $25,000 to $50,000 annually." Better pitch: "America's 4.5 million small-business owners received a potential gift from the tax man last month, as a new law went into effect to double the annual deduction for equipment purchases from $25,000 to $50,000 per year." In the second pitch, the journalist is being given an immediate signal about who would be affected by the story, and can quickly decide if that pertains to the audience.

Pitching: What It Is Not

The newsworthiness of a pitch helps to distinguish it from other types of media outreach with which it is often mistaken, especially press releases. A pitch is a targeted and newsworthy message. A press release is a general message that is sent, shotgun style, to a wide range of media outlets.

Companies should use press releases to make announcements. They are useful when a company needs or wants to issue a public statement about its financial performance, a major personnel change, headquarters relocation, acquisition or merger or major product launch. These activities might be of interest to media covering the geographic area in which the business is located, and they might be of interest to trade publications covering that industry. But the press release says little about a company's unique brand attributes, and nothing about important industry trends that affect customers and clients.

Press releases can be part of your media outreach campaign. They are valuable in helping keep your company in front of journalists, and they also are effective at giving a sense of the company's general activity level. Be sure, however, to distinguish them from pitches. Put the title "PRESS RELEASE" right at the top of a press release; this makes it clear to journalists that the information is being widely disseminated, and it is not likely to lead to a unique, groundbreaking article.

Conclusion

Developing a successful pitch or series of pitches requires maintaining attention on the end-goal: a conversation with a media representative about the ideas you have suggested. It is helpful if you put yourself in the mind of the journalist who is receiving your pitch. Is your idea "news"? Does it appeal to the audience of readers or viewers? Does it contain specific details that differentiate it from other stories? Are those ideas linked to the expertise, skills and knowledge that your company possesses?

With those questions in mind, it's time to turn to the actual process: *mastering the pitch*.

Mastering the Pitch

Having thought about your branding, your message, and the desired media outlets, you are now ready to start pitching! The groundwork that we laid in the first few chapters has given you the information to write a great pitch. Now all you have to do is actually do it.

In this chapter we will explain the common format and elements of a great pitch and define critical rules for making each pitch into compelling, targeted story ideas that will appeal to specific audiences and grab the attention of journalists.

The Format

While each pitch is unique, public relations experts have developed a general format for pitches. By adopting this basic format, you can be confident that you will highlight your major points and present yourself as a credible, professional resource for the media.

Look in the Appendices for examples of pitches in a typical format.

The format for your pitch should have four elements, presented in this order: opening paragraph (lede), supporting information, your credentials, and your contact information. Let's look at each element.

Opening paragraph. In the newspaper and magazine business, the first paragraph is known as the lede, which is derived from the lead type used by printers in the 18th, 19th and first half of the 20th centuries. The first paragraph in a news story covers the classic "who, what, when, where, why, how" information.

Your lede does not have to contain all of those elements, but it definitely should include the "what" element. The reason is that you are trying to attract attention to an issue (a "what"), rather than produce the entire article.

Try to answer one of more of these "what" questions in your lede. What is the issue? What is the problem? What is the solution? What is the trend? But remember, do not focus on yourself, or your product or service—focus on the problem and the solution.

EXAMPLE

You are an insurance underwriter and have a new policy for medical professionals. A weak lede would be: "A new insurance policy is available for medical professionals." It does state a "what" issue clearly, but it is not the right issue. Insurance publication readers want to know immediately if the policy might apply to their business.

Instead, your lede should give more information. It should transform the "what" question to "what is the problem that is being solved?" A better lede: Medical professionals are finding it more costly to obtain liability insurance, even while medical litigation has increased to record levels. "Fortunately, new, price-competitive insurance products have the potential to offer solutions for tens of thousands of medical professionals," according to Jennifer Harrison, ChFC, CLU, an independent insurance agent in Thousand Oaks, CA.

The problem is stated first, which grabs the reader's attention. Then a solution is noted. Finally, the person seeking to be contacted is named, and her credentials are listed.

EXAMPLE 2

Continuing with the example of the insurance representative, let's see what happens if Ms. Harrison targets her pitch more specifically to individual media outlets. To pitch to a magazine for dentists, she would use data related to lawsuits that dentists incur, rather than the broader category of medical professionals.

A lede: Malpractice lawsuits against dentists have increased by 10% per year since 2002, and become the number one concern of many professionals across the country. With the spiraling costs of litigation, insurance has become harder—and pricier—to obtain.

"Fortunately, new, price-competitive insurance products have the potential to offer solutions for tens of thousands of dentists," according to Jennifer Harrison, ChFC, CLU, an independent insurance agent in Thousand Oaks, CA. "Combined with creative thinking by an insurance agent, we have found that dentists can reduce their insurance expenditures by $15,000 per year—and improve their coverage."

Supporting information. After the lede, you have a few paragraphs to provide additional information. We recommend no more than four or five paragraphs. This is where you can address additional "who, what, when, where, why, how" aspects related to your idea. In these paragraphs, you must be succinct, but also authoritative. You must provide enough information to show that you know what you are talking about and that the idea is worthy of follow up by the reporter. This might seem like a huge amount of information to cram into a few paragraphs, but remember that you are not trying to write a complete article. You are only trying to generate enough interest so that the reporter will contact you.

Statistics are one of the best ways to support your argument. Statistics carry the weight of fact, and they are succinct. Even better, citing statistics often will lead the reporter to contact you to pursue additional issues that the statistics raise.

Statistics, and any other information that you provide, is best received if it comes from a reputable, well-known third party. This might be a chamber of commerce, a national trade association, a recent survey, or the government. Your goal is to give an indication of the scope and scale of the issue you are raising, while aligning your credibility to that of your source.

You also can be the source of the statistics, if you are presenting original survey results or other data that you have collected. Reporters find original data irresistible. I have worked very effectively with financial advisors who create small-scale surveys of their clients to produce original information that led to excellent media opportunities.

Bullet points are another very valuable technique for displaying supporting information in a concise form that is easy for a reporter to review. You should not, however, overwhelm the reporter with eight or ten bullet points, or long bullets. Your bullets do not even have to be complete sentences—that's the reporter's job.

EXAMPLE

Ms. Harrison, the insurance agent, could use bullets to provide two examples of how the new insurance product saved money for her dentist clients. These would support the opening statements with hard data, and would give the reporter a roadmap to follow to start developing a story.

Your credentials. In one of the paragraphs, you should include a short summary of your credentials. This can be a phrase or a full sentence, but it should not overwhelm the newsworthy points you are trying to make.

Ideally, your credentials will show two things: 1) you have expertise in the field, developed through training, experience, and achievement; and 2) you are on top of the most current developments, including the topic you are pitching.

You can show your expertise by citing your professional credentials and education. Your experience can be quantified by referencing how many years you have been in your field. Your level of achievement can signal in numerous ways, such as your job title (if you are owner or chairman of a business) or awards you have won.

Showing that you have timely information about the topic usually comes through quotes you provide in the pitch. These quotes will emphasize the significance of the problem or opportunity that you outlined in the lede. They bring timeliness, perhaps even urgency, to the situation. The quotes also should indicate that you have developed a solution for the problem or a way to take advantage of the opportunity.

Your contact information. Make sure that your pitch ends with an encouragement for the recipient to contact you for an interview. Include all the ways that you can be contacted—office phone, cell phone, email, fax, and so on. If you are working with a media coordinator (either on a contract basis or through in-house staff), include that person's or business' contact information, too. Make it as easy as possible for the reporter to find you.

Content in the Pitch

Following the pitch format is valuable, but the content of your pitch is even more important. By adhering to the following eight Content Rules for Mastering the Pitch, you can create exciting proposals that will attract and hold the attention of media gatekeepers.

Rule No. 1: Be Compelling A pitch must be exciting and compelling. It must direct the attention of journalists or editors immediately to an issue of prominence and importance in the lives of their readers.

Magazine writers learn to master this technique through editorial devices, such as writing ledes that tell a story or highlight an important detail. The most popular of these ledes often focuses on one person. They know that we, as readers, are curious about other people. Readers want to know how the story turns out for that person, and so we will continue to the article's completion.

> *Jennifer Smith never knew her father. He was shipped out to Vietnam while his wife, Eleanor was pregnant, and he did not return. For 40 years, his fate was unknown, but now answers are starting to emerge.*

> *(or...)*

> *Tom and Debra Johnson thought their accountant made a mistake when he told them that they owed nearly $4,300 in federal taxes this year. Instead, they had waded into the "Twilight Zone" that is America's Alternative Minimum Tax.*

You can do the same thing with your pitch. Start your pitch with a personalization of the details. Set the mood.

The idea is to entice the reader to continue to review the pitch and consider contacting you for more information. Ideally, the journalist will follow your suggestion about a way to approach the story and will give you a chance to build on your idea.

However, remember that you are not writing a novel. You are pitching to the news media, and so your idea must have news value. As outlined in Chapter 4, the value of your pitch is based on its newsworthiness. To be newsworthy it should be timely, unusual, controversial, entertaining, or it should resonate with a majority of the audience.

Obviously, some issues can be illustrated through an anecdote or personal example, and some cannot. In general, if you are pitching a story idea that relates directly to the lifestyles of individuals and their families, you probably can come up with an effective personalized lede. If you are presenting technical or industrial information, you should probably stick to facts and trends.

Also, recognize that every pitch does not lead to a major article. A pitch that leads to a "small" article is worthwhile, too. It is your opening to further contact and converse with that reporter.

Finally, to be compelling, your pitch should present a clear perspective. It should offer definitive solutions and ideas. You should be firm. Do not say that a problem cannot be solved. Why would a journalist want to pursue a story in which your answer is, "Well, we don't really know what to do?"

However, while you want to be definitive, you must be careful not to overreach. Journalists have highly tuned "bullshit detectors." They can sense when someone is exaggerating the benefits of a product or service, or presenting an incomplete picture of a problem. Also, journalists are likely to follow their conversations with you by contacting other people in your field. So, if they challenge your statements, ultimately your credibility may suffer. A good way to balance between being definitive and wishy-washy in your pitch is to say that the solution(s) you are offering are only some of the possible options. In an interview or email exchange, you explain why you prefer your solution to other solutions.

Rule No. 2: Be Succinct State your point clearly in the lede; make your supporting statements clearly in a few more paragraphs; and end by indicating your willingness to be contacted for more information.

Don't worry that you can't give a reporter the entire story in a pitch. Your goal is to have a reporter, editor, or news producer send you an email or pick up the phone and say, "Can I talk with you about that idea you sent to me?"

When you think about it, you will realize that you don't want to tell the whole story in your pitch. You want the reporter to call you, or to send an email. You want the opportunity to add more information and to build a relationship as a trusted source. You want to have a chance to find out what else the reporter is writing about, and to explain why you can be a great resource on those subjects, too.

Rule No. 3: Offer Exclusivity When Possible Journalists operate in a highly competitive environment. They are always seeking to be the first to "break" a story. If you can offer them a way to beat their competition—to be the first to cover an issue, or to cover it with a new perspective—you will be much more likely to have your pitch positively received.

There are two forms of exclusivity that you can offer. The first would be to approach a single media outlet with your pitch, and make it clear that their organization is your preferred media outlet. Your pitch letter can even state that you are offering this idea to the outlet "exclusively" or "first." If that outlet declines to pursue the story, contact your second choice, and so on. This method can be time-consuming, but it enables you to build strong relationships with individual members of the media.

The second method is to pitch variations of the same idea to different, even competing, publications. This is more efficient, because you can send the pitch to multiple outlets simultaneously. Also, if you have good media rapport and a good idea, often you can obtain coverage in multiple places.

However, this second method has its challenges, too. You do not want to anger media representatives by making them feel as if you are offering the same "exclusive" story to their competitors. You have to be very careful to ensure that the comments you make are, in fact, different.

There's no quicker way to lose your rapport than to have your "exclusive" show up in competing publications at the same time.

Even if you are pitching a single idea, you can think about offering the pitch to very different publications at the same time. It's possible that your idea will appeal to both consumer media and industry media, but in different ways. If you would like to see your idea picked up by a couple of outlets, simply rework it for the consumer and other professionals in your industry.

EXAMPLE

In Chapter 1, I wrote about Michael Scarborough and his recognition as a 401(k) guru. Scarborough's investment methodology has applications for both individual investors and financial professionals who have large numbers of clients. So Scarborough's media outreach targets both the consumer finance press and also the professional financial press. With the consumer press, he emphasizes the ease of using his system to protect and balance 401(k) accounts; with the financial press, he emphasizes the sophistication of the investing options.

One mistake I often see with new clients is that they have initiated a public relations effort, but it is solely focused on either the consumer or the industry press. Usually, there are fruitful avenues for both types of media. Business owners who serve consumers seem to think that only the consumer press is worth pursuing, but they could not be

If sending a pitch out to several reporters, always send individual emails, never mass emails. Due to the competitive nature of the media business, reporters will not cover a story that they know will be covered by their competitors at the same time and in the same way.

Some public relations firms will try to be efficient by sending the same pitch to numerous reporters by using the bcc (blind copy) function. This hides the identities of other each email recipient from the others. While the bcc function does preserve anonymity, it does not overcome the basic flaw that a single pitch is being sent to different reporters who each have unique perspectives.

more mistaken. Consumers want to know they are working with the best possible provider of a service or product, and nothing is more of a testament to that excellence than recognition in the "trade" publications in your industry.

Rule No. 4: Know Your Recipient When producing variations of a pitch for different media outlets, make sure that you tailor each one to the specialty of that outlet. It is crucial that you know who is on the receiving end of your pitch.

Prior to your pitch, research the publication or electronic media outlet and its editorial focus. It is absolutely crucial that you are a regular reader of the publication or viewer/listener of the show. Not only will you learn about the general topics that the media covers, but you can be sure that you are not pitching an idea that the media outlet just covered. Alternatively, if the outlet has just provided a great deal of coverage on a topic, but you have a different angle on it, you will know what you need to emphasize in your pitch.

You also can learn a great deal about the media outlet's style by becoming a regular reader, viewer or listener. Is it informal or formal? Are issues covered in-depth, or are they quickly summarized? Does the publication or show use a lot of industry lingo, or does it try to speak to a general audience? You need to be aware of these nuances, both in your pitch and for responding when a reporter contacts you.

If possible, do the pre-contact work to become familiar with the reporter or reporters who are your targets. Does that person prefer contact by email or by phone? Is that person "on deadline" on Wednesdays? Sometimes, it is difficult to find out this type of preferred contact information until you have had your first positive response from that reporter. So, during that first phone call or email, make sure you ask the reporter, "What's the best way to get in contact with you in the future? And when are good times to reach you?"

Rule No. 5: *Identify Relevant Audience in the Pitch* Your pitch is aimed at a particular audience, just as the media outlet you are contacting serves a particular subscriber base. Make it clear in your pitch who you think will find the story to be interesting and valuable. Don't force reporters to guess about the link between your pitch and their audiences.

If your pitch has local interest, say so. If your pitch has industry-wide interest, say so. If your pitch is related to current national trends or news stories, then say that, too.

Rule No. 6: *Don't Self-Promote* Although it is important to refer to your credentials, make sure that your pitch does not exceed the boundaries by becoming self-promotional. The pitch is not about you—it is about an idea that you wish to share with the media and with the outlet's readership or audience. (If you have won an award or received a promotion, a press release might be appropriate.)

When reading pitches, editors and reporters only want to know how you can be helpful to them. How can you help them educate their readers? How can you help them excite or entertain their readers? Those are the types of questions you need to answer in your pitch. If the pitch results in a phone call or email, then you can display the full depth of your intelligence to the reporter.

Rule No. 7: Real Life Sells As noted earlier, real-life stories and anecdotes are very powerful communicators. By referencing specific people and their specific problems, a reporter draws in the readers, and keeps them to the finish. A pitch should signal to a reporter that you can provide real-life anecdotes and examples that will resonate with the audience.

How do you introduce a real-life aspect to a pitch? The easiest way is to provide two or three examples of people who are affected by the problem or trend in your pitch. These people give a reporter a sense of the issue's potential impact.

If you are going to develop a pitch that focuses on individuals, you must be able to follow up with more details about individualized cases. If you are in a business that works with individuals (financial advisor, insurance, attorney, accountant, personal trainer, etc.), arrange ahead of time to have clients ready to talk with a reporter.

You also can provide real-life insights through other types of examples that illustrate a problem and a solution. An engineering business might describe its innovative use of structural steel to reduce the cost of a new building. An airline might refer to passenger's frustrations with delays, and then explain how it has created a new solution.

Rule No. 8: Don't Send Attachments Like everyone else, reporters are deluged with email, and, as a profession, they probably lead the world in per-person spam. The reason for this is fairly obvious: their names and contact information are in the public domain. The email addresses of print reporters are usually noted alongside their articles, and the email addresses of electronic media reporters are noted when their reports are linked to web sites.

The prevalence and potential harm from spam make reporters very reluctant to open unsolicited email attachments. You will do much better if you cut-and-paste your pitch into the body of an email, instead of sending the pitch as an attachment.

Within the body of the email, you should provide a link to your web site. The link will enable the reporter to learn a little more about you and your organization before contacting you about your pitch.

Finding Ideas for Pitches

Great ideas for pitches can come from anywhere. Be ready:

- Your clients and customers

- Newspapers, magazines, TV, radio reports

- The Web

- Your community

- Industry trends

- Develop an annual survey of your clients (original research always sells)

- Think outside the box

Your Weekly Pitch Strategy

Do you think it's impossible to come up with a great pitch each week? Here's how you can do it.

- Listen to what your best resources -- clients and customers -- are talking about. Almost always, the media will be interested, too.

- Keep a pad of paper by the phone. Write down all interesting questions on the pad.

- At the end of the week, review the pad, and pick the two questions that were the most interesting or unique.

- Research the questions.

- Write the pitch.

- Call the customer and ask if they can be contacted.

- Send out the pitch!

The Pitch Timeline

Distributing a pitch to the media takes preparation and careful planning. Rarely can you type a random story idea and throw it out to the mass media, and expect any type of positive response. You need to: refine your pitch, create your targeted media list, determine the best mode of distribution, distribute the pitch, do the necessary follow-up work, and follow up after the interview, story, or event. Careful planning and execution will significantly improve your chances of success.

Of course, planning and execution takes time. To pitch effectively, you need to think well in advance of when you hope to see a story about what you're pitching. As the following examples indicate, your pitch cycle can be any where from 10 days to 10 weeks long.

Pitching a Random Story Idea Story pitches based on your observations about current news events are the quickest cycle, and they are the least rigid in form and content. There may be no right time or wrong time to distribute these, but they should be highly timely and meet several of the five qualifiers of newsworthiness.

Once you have developed the pitch and identified your targeted media outlets and reporters, begin pitching. We recommend pitching stories of this caliber over a short period of time, or less than two weeks. If the story is not picked up in that period, chances are that it does not carry the interest that you anticipated. A reporter might contact you at a later date, but it's time for you to move on to your next project.

Sample Random Story Idea Pitch Timeline (Ten-day schedule)

Day One – Ensure pitch is organized appropriately and identify targeted media as Level A Targets, Level B Targets, and Level C Targets.

Day Two – Distribute pitch to Level A Targets via desired modes of communication (i.e., phone, fax, email, and "snail" mail).

Day Three – Allow the pitch to simmer as the initial targets may have been on deadline, etc.

Day Four – Follow up accordingly with either an email or, if appropriate, a phone call. Identify interest and prepare distribution for Level B Targets.

Day Five – Distribute pitch to Level B Targets via desired modes of communication (i.e., phone, fax, email, "snail" mail).

Day Six – Allow the pitch to simmer as the initial targets may have been on deadline, etc.

Day Seven – Follow up accordingly with either an email or, if appropriate, a phone call. Identify interest and prepare distribution for Level C Targets.

Day Eight – Distribute pitch to Level C Targets via desired modes of communication (i.e., phone, fax, email, "snail" mail).

Day Nine – Allow the pitch to simmer as the initial targets may have been on deadline, etc.

Day Ten – Follow up accordingly with either an email or, if appropriate, a phone call. Identify interest.

Sample Event Pitch Timeline (timeline varies)

At the other end of the spectrum, you might be organizing a conference or gala fundraiser, or you might be trying to develop interest in the opening of a new store location. For these types of pitches, you need to prepare for a longer, more intensive pitch series. You also will send your pitches to a much wider scope of possible reporters, editors, and other interested parties. Your PR campaign will be intimately tied with your traditional marketing campaign, as you are seeking to "touch" potential attendees, customers, donors, or supporters through a variety of media—which creates a powerful and positive impression.

The pitch for an event or a charitable cause does not rise or fall on the newsworthiness as much as it does on the overall interest to the audience of readers and viewers. If you are fortunate and savvy, you might even create enough of a buzz to make your event newsworthy!

Note that the following timeline also incorporates post-event follow-up. Include everything so you won't miss the details you will be promoting to the media. This is crucial to your overall media strategy, as you want to ensure that the media is eager to hear about your next activity, too.

The following is an actual event promotional timeline that Perception Inc., developed for Dan Taylor, creator of The Parent Care Solution and author of *The Parent Care Conversation*. His idea was to create a National Parent Care Day to get the word out about his work in the parent care arena.

Feb. 6 – Solidify date for National Parent Care Day

Feb. 13 – Press release sent to media regarding National Parent Care Day

Mar. 1 – Promotional packages sent to governors, mayors, and U.S. legislators seeking proclamations declaring it National Parent Care Day on May 22nd across the country

Mar. 11 – Follow-up calls placed to governors and mayors following up on the requests that were sent a week earlier

Mar. 15 – Proclamations begin arriving. Develop a spreadsheet of proclamations and begin to identify key media outlets in those states and metropolitan areas

Mar 16 to Apr. 1 – Continue to collect proclamations and begin to lay out the schedule of events for National Parent Care Day, including:

- Potential press conferences and photo ops with governors and mayors – finalize details

- Seminar/workshop/town hall style meeting – finalize details

- Prepare all press releases/pitches/advisories

Apr. 1 – Distribute press releases to key media outlets in states and metropolitan areas where proclamations were received. Provide detail on the proclamations with quotes from those governors and mayors

Apr. 2 to Apr. 13 – Finalize National Parent Care Day details and prepare national press release with details of the day

Apr. 14 – Press release distributed to national media covering the events planned for National Parent Care Day

Apr. 20 – Follow up with media via desired mode of communication to identify interest, coverage, etc

Apr. 22 – Contact all event/calendar editors to have the event(s) listed in the Community Calendar sections of the local/state newspapers

May 1 – Finalize details for joint press conference with the mayor of xxxx city and follow-up reception

May 2 – Develop pitch on the increasing need for parent care in the U.S. Ensure pitch is organized appropriately and a targeted media list is organized by Level A Targets, Level B Targets, and Level C Targets.

May 3 – Pitch is distributed to Level A Targets via desired modes of communication (i.e., phone, fax, email, "snail" mail).

May 4 – Allow the pitch to simmer as the initial targets may have been on deadline, etc.

May 5 – Follow up accordingly with either an email or, if appropriate, a phone call. Identify interest and prepare distribution for Level B Targets.

May 6 – Pitch is distributed to Level B Targets via desired modes of communication (i.e., phone, fax, email, "snail" mail).

May 10 – Allow the pitch to simmer as the initial targets may have been on deadline, etc.

May 11 – Follow up accordingly with either an email or, if appropriate, a phone call. Identify interest and prepare distribution for Level C Targets.

May 12 – Pitch is distributed to Level C Targets via desired modes of communication (i.e., phone, fax, email, "snail" mail).

May 13 – Allow the pitch to simmer as the initial targets may have been on deadline, etc.

May 14 – Follow up accordingly with either an email or, if appropriate, a phone call. Identify interest.

May 15 – Press advisory sent inviting media to National Parent Care Day press conference with the mayor of xxx city

May 16-22 – Interviews arranged for Dan Taylor with national media outlets to discuss the growing importance of parent care in the U.S.

May 20 – Press advisory sent inviting media to National Parent Care Day press conference with the mayor of xxx city

May 22 – National Parent Care Day

- Conduct press conference

- Hold seminar/workshop/town hall style event

May 29 – Follow-up with media attendees, offering additional information if needed.

Pitching Through the Eyes of Journalists

Just as you try to be the best possible financial advisor, attorney, physician, salesperson, building contractor, or fast food franchise owner you can be…members of the media try to do the best they can. No matter your line of work, you need to be able to depend on other people to provide you with sound advice and service so you can do your job effectively.

Let's say you own a business that requires you to have printed literature available at conferences and events throughout your given industry. You probably would depend on outside vendors of printing services to provide you with the best possible rates and timely delivery so you can be at your next event ready to go. Journalists are no different. They rely on outside vendors of information (you) and need to know that what you are selling (your facts, viewpoints, and opinions) is reliable, timely, and will help them do their jobs better.

When you make journalists' lives easier and their articles better, you have launched strong partnerships that are "win-win" situations. Building those partnerships—any partnership—requires understanding the perspective of the other party. One of the goals of this book is to bring you inside the heads of journalists, and to teach you how to think about pitching from the perspective of the journalists you are trying to reach.

In this chapter, we will go further into the journalists' world. We will hear from them—directly and in their own words—about how they view pitches for news and feature articles. We will learn when they are most receptive to pitches from business owners, marketing directors, technical experts, and PR representatives. We will learn what appeals to journalists, and what turns them off instantly. Through an in-depth survey developed specially for this book, we will find out exactly what to approach journalists with and how to approach them.

Let's get started.

Listen to Your Market

As a successful business leader, you listen to your market. You spend much time and effort trying to learn what your customers and prospects want from your company, and how you can best provide it. If you're like most successful business leaders, you:

- read industry publications
- attend conferences and trade shows
- conduct surveys of customers
- talk to your suppliers
- generate internal sales representative feedback
- hire consultants

You should treat your target audience of journalists in exactly the same manner. Think of them as customers. Though they will not pay you in cash, the compensation they provide in the form of positive publicity can be worth a great deal to your company.

In late 2006 and early 2007, my business, Perception, Inc., conducted an in-depth survey in which more than 100 active journalists told us in great detail what makes an effective pitch and pitching strategy. We asked them all the questions that you need to know in order to develop an effective and sustainable pitching program. How do journalists wish to be contacted? When do they wish to be contacted?

What topics catch their attention? What information has no interest for them? Answers to those questions, and much more, are addressed in this chapter and the remainder of the book.

The journalists who responded to the nationwide survey represent a cross-section of experienced, high-impact information leaders who you want to reach. The median journalism experience level of respondents was 20-22 years. Respondents work for major business publications, such as *BusinessWeek*, *Crain's*, and the *Dow Jones News Wire*. They work at top online information providers, such as *CNBC.com* and *MSN*.com. They also produce news and feature programming for local and national television and radio, and represent each of the four network affiliates across the nation, as well as cable television.

Respondents' primary beats ranged from business news and personal finance, to entertainment, to politics, to health issues. One respondent's beat is the comics and online gaming industry, which indicates that whatever business you are in, there's a journalist already writing about it.

True to form, many journalists in the survey said that their beats are "everything," which reflects the growing pressure on journalists to expand their knowledge base in a competitive, fast-paced environment. Treat this as an opportunity for you: journalists who have to cover a wide range of issues are even more reliant than ever before on outside experts.

Our survey results were definitive and insightful. Overall, we confirmed that journalists utilize a vast network of sources for their story ideas and development. They constantly prowl for information and analysis in their beats, as well as for articles on related areas of interest. Journalists seek to anticipate the next trend in their field, so that they can keep their readers on the cutting edge.

Journalists rely on regular sources most heavily, but in the survey, they confirmed that they are always eager to expand their network. We can conclude that if you wish to become part of that network of trusted sources, you can build a relationship based on providing quality, relevant information in a timely manner.

The results of the survey's key questions are presented and discussed below.

QUESTION 1: WHAT IS YOUR PREFERRED METHOD OF BEING CONTACTED?

(Percentage of respondents)
Email: 83
Phone: 10
United States mail: 5
Fax: 1

Overwhelmingly, journalists prefer contact by email. This is not surprising, given the speed with which journalists (and most of the rest of us in the business world) operate today.

From a journalist's perspective, one of the best attributes of email is that it can be accessed from anywhere. Journalists often lead professional lives similar to those of business executives or sales people with large territories. They constantly move: to conferences and trade shows, press briefings, and one-on-one interviews. During travel or downtime between events, journalists avidly check their electronic communications devices.

Therefore, you will find that it's usually easiest to reach a journalist by email. Given journalists' schedules, you might receive a response at the unlikeliest time, or from an unexpected place. That's just the nature of the news business today. You might send an email pitch at noon, and not hear from the TV producer for several days. Then, a quick inquiry will show up on your email, dated at 3:45 AM from London, where the journalist has been attending an international trade show. Your correspondent might ask you to contact a co-producer in New York to arrange for a quick phone interview later that same day, referencing two new trends that the journalist noticed at the trade expo a half world away.

Even if you are working with local media, you will find that journalists have unusual schedules. Often, a news reporter will return your email at 10 PM or 11 PM, during a dull part of a hearing at a city council office.

While email is wonderfully convenient, all of us understand that email is an imperfect communications medium. We all have heard stories about people in business and government (and in their personal lives) who have found trouble through sloppy email practices. It's the same when you work with journalists online. Poor email etiquette will undermine your relationship and potentially cause embarrassment.

Use good email practices when writing your pitch, and especially when following up with online answers to a reporter's questions. Be thoughtful in your response. Be polite. Don't use slang or emoticon symbols. Most importantly, assume that your email is not private, even if you have been assured that it is.

QUESTION 2: IF SOMEONE WANTS TO PITCH A STORY TO YOU, WHAT IS THE QUICKEST AND BEST WAY TO DO IT?

(Percentage of respondents)
Email with a few bullet points: 68
Email with a lot of detail: 15
U.S. mail in letter form: 5
Fax with a few bullet points: 3
Fax with a lot of detail: 0
Phone call: 10

In their answers, journalists confirmed that they prefer to receive pitches by email, and they added that short pitches clearly highlighting the key points are the best way to attract attention. Email pitches using bullet points have become the *de facto* standard. Look at the examples throughout this book and in the appendix for models of how to write a concise, easy-to-read pitch.

If journalists prefer short, bullet-point pitches, why did 15 percent of respondents say that they prefer long emails? My experience in the PR business suggests that these journalists are referring to pitches from trusted sources they have worked with in the past. As a source builds credibility, the reporter will be more open to pitches for more complicated topics that require longer pitches. Often, these are best introduced through a short phone call ("Hi John, this is Pamela. I'm going to send you some information about which Xbox games are most popular with teenage girls. It might be an interesting story."), and then the email follow-up.

In my experience, journalists will rarely read long, detailed pitches from unknown sources. They simply do not have the time.

QUESTION 3: TIME OF DAY THAT IS BEST TO CALL

(Percentage of respondents – multiple answers allowed)
No preferred time: 34
8 to 10 AM: 33
10 to 11 AM: 51
11 AM to NOON: 31
1 to 2 PM: 28
2 to 3 PM: 31
3 to 4 PM: 20
4 to 5 PM: 19
After 5 PM: 8

Of all the questions on the survey, this one received the most widely dispersed response. If you look closely, in fact, the responses add up to much more than 100 percent. This is because many participants provided more than one answer.

Although the responses might not seem to exhibit any patterns at first, their message begins to take shape when you look closely. Journalists' schedules vary according to many factors. Some journalists have multiple deadlines during the day, and they are most prominently represented by the 34 percent who did not list a preferred time. These journalists simply do not know how their workflow will occur on any given day. They constantly encounter unexpected events or interview opportunities, based on activities that occur within their beat. Your pitch could come at a good time for them, or a bad time. If it's a bad time, they will ignore it until they have a respite. This is why they find email to be so effective; they can archive your message and respond when it is most convenient.

The survey also indicates those journalists who do have a preference about contact time. They like to receive news pitches early in the day, before they are too tied up with the day's reporting and other responsibilities. Again, this makes sense. If you are a business owner, you probably use the earliest hours of the day to take care of your own outreach activities and long-term projects, in advance of the "crisis of the day" that will soon demand most of your attention.

The journalists who responded that they prefer late-afternoon contacts are typically reporters who work on daily deadlines in TV or newspapers. These reporters, editors, and producers have to complete their work by mid-afternoon deadlines, so that their pieces can be fitted into the puzzle that is a newscast or a daily newspaper – while leaving time for rewrites, editing, and last-minute adjustments. The schedule for these journalists is to come in at the start of the day, facing five or six hours to complete their assignments. They do not wish to be interrupted during these prime hours, especially as their deadlines draw close. But after deadline, while they are winding down the day's business, they start to prepare for their next assignments. That is when they have a few minutes to consider your pitch.

These numbers suggest that, in general, morning is better than afternoon. Yet, the overall data hides an important fact: Most journalists do have strong preferences for when they would like to be contacted. You will have to find out what their preference is on a case-by-case basis, as you get to know them through your initial pitching outreach. I have found that the best way to learn a journalist's preference is to ask when you first get an email or phone response to a pitch. Make it clear that you want to be helpful in the way that is most convenient to the journalist, and you will quickly start to develop all-crucial rapport.

QUESTION 4: DO YOU HAVE AN ASSISTANT/ ASSOCIATE?

(Percentage of respondents)
Yes: 12
No: 88

Only a few journalists have assistants or associates working for them, taking calls, and relaying messages. Most journalists work on their own. Editors and upper-level news producers often have assistants, who help coordinate inquiries, but those people are usually not your primary pitching targets anyway.

The fact that journalists do not have assistants does not mean that they work in a vacuum. Within a publication or media outlet, reporters on staff usually collaborate up the chain of command, as they submit articles to sub-editors and editors. They then revise their articles, based on input from above, and often will ask for advice from their colleagues (such as good reference material about a topic or a trusted source for a quote). But the work belongs to a single journalist most of the time.

A newspaper, magazine, or television program is a team effort, but it is one in which people typically make individual contributions. A baseball team might be a good analogy. Baseball is a team sport. Yet, individual batters do most of the work against a single pitcher. The cumulative performance of the batters, one at a time, generates runs. Consider the contrast with football, in which each play is dependent on the simultaneous interactions of all or most of the 11 players on the field.

The good news is that a journalist's lack of staff assistants and associates makes your pitching easier. You do not have to fight through layers of bureaucracy to reach your intended contact. You can go right to the reporter, through email and/or telephone, and offer your ideas and services.

QUESTION 5: WHAT TYPES OF STORIES AND STORY IDEAS ARE YOU SEEKING FROM SOURCES?

This was an open-ended question, but we have grouped the responses into general categories. Again, the figures add up to more than 100 percent, due to many reporters who cover multiple topics (sometimes for multiple media outlets).

(Percentage of respondents)

Lifestyle trends *(entertainment, homes, cooking, and celebrities)***:** 16
Local news and features: 15
Investing/personal finance: 15
Industry trends: 11
Legislation/politics: 10
Industry-specific news: 9
Case studies/applications of technologies: 7
Corporate finance: 7
Human interest: 7
Sharp, edgy, surprising stories: 5
IT security and privacy: 5
Real estate: 5
New products: 3
Internet-related: 3
Education: 3
Miscellaneous *(includes how-to or tutorial, healthcare, energy, and the Hispanic market)***:** 10

The responses to this question yield many interesting insights. The first observation is that members of the media cover a wide range of subjects. It would be hard for your business or organization to be involved in activities that do not interest many media outlets and reporters. You might have to work a little bit to find the right ones, but you can be confident that they exist.

The survey answers also indicate that the topics with the greatest interest to the media span a wide range, but they can be loosely grouped under the heading of topics with an immediate impact on people's lives. The top three categories on our survey each speak directly to individuals and their daily concerns and interests: lifestyle, local news, and investments. This is why we emphasize that your pitch must relate to people on an individual level, whenever possible. For example, a pitch for a new mutual fund investment should be about which types of people will benefit from investing in the fund, not about how the investments are selected. A well-crafted pitch will not leave it up to journalists to make the connection to how the topic will relate to their audiences.

Most likely you have noticed that celebrity and entertainment news scored high on the survey. What does this mean? In the introduction to this book, I argued that seeking celebrity status is often an empty achievement—the clichéd 15 minutes of fame earned by Kato Kaelin and hundreds of other forgettable characters. But it seems that journalists are saying in this survey that they do write about celebrities. The difference is that in this survey, journalists are saying that if your product or service is linked to a celebrity of current interest, they might use this as the "hook" to attract their readers. The journalists are not suggesting that you need to be a celebrity, nor that celebrity trumps substance. If you can use celebrities to link to your product or service, you might have a stronger pitch—but you still need to have something valuable to say.

In addition to sharing information about the topics they seek, the survey respondents commented on more general content aspects of a preferred pitch. For example, several journalists noted that they like pitches with surprising or counterintuitive ideas. These ideas will grab the attention of the readers and make them want to read the article to find out more information. Similarly, respondents noted that articles describing industry trends for the business community are highly popular, because business success often correlates with being ahead of the trend.

QUESTION 6: WHAT ARE YOUR BIGGEST PET PEEVES WHEN IT COMES TO STORY PITCHING AND BEING CONTACTED?

(Percentage of respondents – multiple responses allowed)
People do not understand what is newsworthy: 59
Pitches are advertorial...not editorial: 53
Pitches do not fit my beat: 42
Pitches are too long: 30
Calling at the wrong time of day: 19
People do not know how I prefer to receive pitches: 8
Other: 24

Like everyone else, journalists have pet peeves. There are good ways and bad ways to approach reporters. Most of the responses above are fairly commonsensical, and they are typical for all of us who have busy careers and lives.

While most journalists are receptive to pitches, it's easy to decipher from the responses that sending information of low value is the quickest way to join the "reject" pile. Newsworthiness is at the top of a journalist's priority list, and it's why we outlined The Four Criteria of News in Chapter 4.

Closely related to newsworthiness is a journalist's expectation that a pitch is a genuine editorial idea, not a disguised advertisement. Journalists understand that you are contacting them to promote yourself and your business, and they respect your desire to raise your profile with their readers. A certain amount of self-promotion is allowed in a pitch. But when a pitch focuses solely on you – when it lacks information of value to the outside world – then it is advertorial. It is an effort to manipulate the journalist, and it will be rejected.

The responses also note the importance of matching a reporter's beat. Inevitably, you will send pitches to reporters who are not covering your beat. Even if the reporter covered you in the past, beats change on a regular basis. Be attuned to what the reporter is covering, and be prepared to update your contact list regularly.

The "other" response to this question yielded remarks that included:

- "People do not understand what our magazine covers, [and then they] continue to call to follow up"

- "People call to ask questions that could be answered by looking at our Web Site"

- "Calling on my deadline days"

- "Pitching a client, not a story"

- "…sending pitches to a gazillion people on our staff, hoping one will hit"

- "'Shotgun' pitches that cover too many topics"

- "Not telling me about how the impact is felt by my readers…"

- "I intensely dislike being hounded. If I say a pitch doesn't work for us, that's because it doesn't work for us!"

- "Pitches that come too late for my deadlines"

We will present more comments from journalists about what they want and dislike in pitches in our next chapters.

QUESTION 7: HOW DO YOU FEEL A PITCH SHOULD BE DEVELOPED FOR YOU TO TAKE NOTICE?

(Percentage of respondents – multiple responses allowed)
Bullet points with details: 70
Facts and statistics: 61
Real stories and anecdotes: 61
Enticing introduction: 49
Known expert or authority: 32
A quote from the expert or authority: 21

The responses emphasize many of the key components to a good pitch that we have covered throughout this book: use of facts, interesting stories, strong lead paragraphs, and reference to independent experts.

Journalists must work quickly, often scanning an email in seconds to decide if it contains information of value to their readers. They are looking for statements from you about who is affected by the topic you are pitching, what the key facts are that you can share, and whether you have objective data and expert opinion to back up your statement.

A single pitch cannot cover every possible benefit of your product or service, nor can it reference every type of customer who can benefit. Remember that a pitch is a targeted effort. Do not try the shotgun approach of making broad claims that your product or service is the best for everyone. Select your target market, and focus on it. You are trying to uncover that nugget which will grab the attention of a slice of a publication's readership, and lead to a phone call or email in return.

QUESTION 8: WHAT DO YOU LOOK FOR IN A RESOURCE'S PROFESSIONAL BACKGROUND AND/OR EXPERIENCE?

(Percentage of respondents – multiple responses allowed)
Authority figure within their respective company: 60
Personal history and rapport with you and your outlet: 56
Years of experience in the industry: 55
Noted author/presenter on the subject matter: 29
Advanced degrees and/or professional licenses/designations: 20
A lot of experience working with the media: 18

This question really asks journalists how they decide which sources to trust. Facing an onslaught of press releases and pitches each week, journalists must develop a hierarchy of contacts. Through technical experience and personal interactions, certain people rise to the top of that list.

In fact, the responses to this question indicate a very even balance between your credentials, your experience, and the rapport that you have started to build with the journalist. This makes sense. Journalists need to work with experts because journalists are not experts. Also, journalists need to work with people who are easy to work with. An expert is not valuable if he or she is never available for a comment, or misses deadlines, or says that information is proprietary and cannot be shared publicly.

Clearly, you need to have both technical expertise and interpersonal skills. It's the same formula that has served you well as you have prospered in your profession and business.

Conclusion

The major data points in our survey reinforce the ideas in this book. Journalists respond positively to pitches delivered through email with newsworthy, short, attention-grabbing information. Journalists cover almost every topic imaginable, and regardless of the business you are trying to promote, you will find members of the media who are eager to hear from you. Finally, journalists will judge you based on both your credentials/expertise and the ease with which they can work with you.

CHAPTER 7

The Best of Pitching

I n Chapter 6, journalists from across the United States shared information about how to pitch to them. They discussed their preferred times and forms of contact; their primary beats and more topics they track; how to attract their attention (and avoid their anger!); and what credentials they find impressive.

In this chapter, we look at how to "click" with a journalist in even greater detail. Journalists share stories about the best pitches that they have received from both PR professionals and business entrepreneurs. What attracted their attention? How did a pitch communicate its relevance? How much information is enough—and what detail is irrelevant?

In their own words, here is what journalists say makes a great pitch.

Content

THINK AHEAD

- "A PR firm saw we had an international investing story on our editorial calendar in three months. They called me...and offered two international fund managers to interview." – *Editor, national consumer finance publication*

- "A recent pitch for a December 2006 The Learning Channel series premiere was introduced nicely (I'm familiar with the contact, and she made the intro a little personal). She detailed the show, and whether or not art, interviews, and screening tapes would be available, and when. The release came by e-mail, and was well in time for our deadlines." – *Entertainment reviewer, major metropolitan newspaper chain*

- "The best pitches are ones that show that the writer or PR person finds a 'fit' to my published editorial calendar." – *Editor, trade newspaper for electronics industry*

KNOW YOUR AUDIENCE

- "Anything that shows an understanding of what we are likely to publish. I'm less concerned with the presentation, as long as the idea is on target." – *Publisher, lifestyle magazine with marine focus*

- "The pitcher should know what I like, and the pitch should be about one line. It doesn't matter how much free stuff you give me, or how many pages the package is. Either I want it or I don't." – *Producer, national radio news service*

- "The best pitches are ones where the sender has read the magazine and understands exactly the kind of information that our readers are looking for. Sometimes it's about a timely topic, and sometimes it's just an offer to act as a resource on an issue that interests our readers. In many cases, I won't be writing about the topic immediately, but I will keep good resources in my background files for future articles." – *Editor, national consumer finance magazine and Website*

- "Any story pitch that shows the publicist is familiar with our newscast; a pitch that clearly has the date, time, location, and contact info prominently featured; any pitch that can be conveyed in two or three sentences." – *Reporter, Fox television affiliate*

- "The best pitches are very narrowly focused to our readers/audience. I get a lot of pitches that are very widely shot-gunned. The PR person should do a little homework when making a pitch and have a good idea who my audience is before making the pitch." – *Editor, small daily newspaper*

GET TO THE POINT

- "It was e-mailed, it was brief, it was legitimately newsworthy, and it had attachments that allowed me to drill down into the subject when I had the chance. It also made a relevant person available." – *Business reporter, national newswire service*

- "A good pitch almost reads like a news brief…granted, one that's most likely filled with complimentary quotes and overstated adjectives. My best advice: Keep it short, and keep it interesting. If you can't write something that's somewhat compelling, why should I waste my time with the story?" – *Editor, government regulation newsletter*

- "A good pitch … can be summarized in a couple of sentences. Tell me what you've got and why it's important to our readers. It can be a phone call or an email. I don't need the story written for me, I just need the news angle." – *Publisher of multiple business newspapers*

- "…be concise and focused." – *Publisher, African-American heritage magazine and Website*

- "I received a pitch about a new Website for at-risk teens. The PR rep for the foundation sent an email that was extremely informative and sent me to the Website. It was about four paragraphs in length—short, sweet, and to the point." – *Features reporter, major metropolitan daily newspaper*

- "Offer enough information to show that a valid story exists, but don't overwhelm." – *Freelance journalist*

- "The best are direct. Here's what I have and why it's important to you." – *Reporter, midsized metro market daily newspaper*

- "It was clear, concise, and to the point, and took less than two [para]graphs to convey." – *Reporter, national personal finance magazine*

PROVIDE SOMETHING NEW

- "In general, a pitch that is unique (i.e., not a spam e-mail that was sent to other reporters) and related to the field I cover." – *Editor, oil industry trade publications*

- "A pitch from an expert on a new and complex accounting problem that can wreak havoc with the fixed-income portion of a portfolio." – *Editor, trade publication for financial professionals*

- "Most recent [effective] one hit on all the points of interest for my newsletter, but by offering for consideration a topic we hadn't covered in depth previously. It wasn't too long, made use of bullets to highlight the relevant information, and stressed activities the company was currently engaged in and could show results on." – *Reporter, entertainment industry trade publisher*

- "PR pitched story that fit my beat, was newsworthy, and hadn't been overdone in press already." – *Editor, investment industry trade publication*

BE NEWSWORTHY

- "Pitches that note the news hook…When President Bush signed the pension bill in 2006 [I received an effective pitch about] how it affected viewers…and specific people to be interviewed for the story." – *Editor, cable and web financial news service*

- "I received a call recently [soon after the 2006 fall elections] from a man about a problem involving voting machines. He was knowledgeable and led me to good sources for the story." – *Reporter, major metropolitan daily newspaper*

- "It's short, to the point, and involves an ongoing or recent news peg. It also should be presented in the style of a news story." – *Reporter, major metropolitan daily newspaper*

USE UNIQUE SURVEY DATA

- "I just received this today… 'A new national survey out today finds that America's young workforce is more concerned about paying their cell phone and credit card bills than spending money on health benefits. Approximately 30 percent of 18- to 24-year-olds are uninsured in the United States. Often dropped from their existing coverage at age 19 or when they graduate, young adults are left to find health benefits coverage on their own as they transition to the workforce. According to the new survey, 44 percent of young workers would rather pay their monthly cell phone bill than for health insurance; and 46 percent of young workers without health insurance say they will enroll when they can afford it.' It was followed by a longer release with more details." - *Reporter, major metropolitan daily newspaper*

PRESENT REAL-LIFE INFORMATION AND ANALYSIS

- "A benefits manager (not a PR person) contacted me to tell me about an analysis of his company's disease management program that invalidated claims by the DM vendor that it had reduced healthcare costs. The release read, in part: 'Attached are two reports. The PDF file is [the insurer's] pitch that the DM programs saved us large sums. I am a skeptic—I think DM programs are good to help these very sick people deal with their medical problems, but as far as saving hard dollars, well.... The Excel file is an analysis we had [third parties] prepare that shows, for employees who were covered for a full year (2003) with no DM program and then a full year (2004) in a DM program, what were the average costs and claims paid. As I suspected, even with the DM programs, costs went up. May make an interesting article: Do DM programs really save hard, total dollars?'" – *Editor, national business management magazine*

- "A story on security training exercises used real-life examples and clearly explained how readers would benefit from reading the article." – *Editor, security industry trade publication*

- "Targeted case study aimed at a specific magazine, with loads of contacts to follow up with to flesh out the pitch. [The pitch] came via e-mail, it listed the why and how of the application, it gave contacts both with PR and the lead company (user), with minimal interference of the vendor company. It didn't indicate that the sender would 'be following up with you in a day or so to see your reaction' -- which is a major turn off since I can rarely expect to be ready to discuss in a day or two of receipt." – *Editor, national magazine for audio-visual and photography professionals*

LOCAL RELEVANCE

- "Local hospital was starting innovative bariatric gastric bypass surgery. The pitch told me, briefly, why my viewers might like the story, how I might reach someone to be an example of that story (to be in it, as an interviewee), and where I might get video to support the story." – *News producer, local affiliate of national TV network*

- "An announcement of new money appropriated for more inter-state highway lanes gave sufficient notice to reach local sources; had contact information and best time to reach key sources; knew enough about the development to provide basic information I could use for basis of interview questions." – *Transportation and business reporter, daily newspaper in mid-size metro market*

- "I received a press package created by a candidate for municipal council that included a detailed press release with quotes and background information and a disk containing his picture." – *Political reporter, Canadian daily metro newspaper*

PRESENT A HUMAN INTEREST ANGLE

- "I was pitched a story for our May issue (which Mother's Day falls within) that focused on the principal dancers of the Nevada Ballet Theatre and their roles as mothers. I thought that was brilliant!" - *Reporter, Las Vegas-area lifestyle magazine*

- "Today, I got one from folks with a major national restaurant chain about a special event they were holding for troops about to deploy to Iraq. It was not too commercial and was focused on the event and the troops, not on the business." – *Reporter, local affiliate of national TV network*

The Super Pitch

A reporter at a major national business publication provided the example below. It shows when an extensive, detailed pitch can be effective. This pitch contains many of the best aspects of pitches that were described above: an unusual angle on a timely issue of broad interest (investments); reference to real-life data; an expert; and "regular" people who will discuss how the issue affects them.

This pitch is far more detailed than you would likely provide, but it illustrates the extent to which you can work with the media, after you have built rapport on smaller projects.

Here are the basics of the non-dollar investing story that I am proposing. Working titles could be 'Fear of Falling Dollars' or 'Dollar Phobic Investing.'

It used to be that direct international investing was the province of wealthy financiers or risky stock speculators chasing fast money. Now growing ranks of Main Street American investors are looking abroad, not to get rich quick, but to keep what they have worked so hard to achieve. These largely conservative investors have lost faith in the pre-eminence of the U.S. markets and cast a wary eye on the mounting debt that is fueling the American economy.

To achieve true diversification and protection against a major meltdown in the U.S. dollar, these investors are allocating 25%, 50% or even 90% of their portfolios to conservatively-valued, high dividend-paying foreign stocks. Some of these asset types include: New Zealand Property Trusts, Australian mining stocks (Uranium, Nickel, Copper), European oil service stocks, Canadian energy trusts, Far Eastern electric utilities and telecoms, and tanker and transportation stocks.

More immediately, the resumption in the decline in the U.S. dollar will likely begin in earnest after the Fed has signaled the end to its current tightening cycle (which most expect will come in August or perhaps September). When the Fed stops, the dollar will likely fall for two reasons. 1) The Fed will have paused while the ECB and BoJ are still tightening. This will compress the yield differential between U.S. Treasury's and foreign bonds, diminishing the incentives for foreigners to buy dollars. 2) When the Fed demonstrates its unwillingness to risk a recession in order to fully stamp out inflation, inflation will more firmly take root, diminishing the value of dollar-based assets in comparison with non-dollar alternatives.

To prepare for this scenario, savvy investors like Warren Buffett and Bill Gross are recommending a much greater exposure to non-dollar assets, especially those that derive their income from non-dollar sources. Capital Investors (company name changed), puts this idea into practice for rank and file American Investors.

Below are descriptions of three clients of Capital Investors. All of the people described below would be willing to talk to you about why they are looking to move large portions of their portfolios overseas, and how their current investment income has moved up dramatically as a result of buying high yielding foreign assets…[Detailed one-paragraph descriptions of three clients followed.]

I am trying to get access to more people.

The firm is led by Steve Johnson (name changed), *who is a well-known market and economic commentator in print and broadcast media. For more on Steve, check out this BusinessWeek video from this past May.*

Please let me know if this is something you may be interested in. Thanks.

Follow-up

A good idea, pitched to a relevant audience, is essential to a winning pitch. But that is only half of the job. You need to support that newsworthy, well-written pitch with effective personal contact. Treat reporters with respect when you send the pitch (preferred deadlines, mode of contact, etc.), and when you respond to their requests for interviews and additional information.

Below are examples of the type of support that journalists praise.

THINK CREATIVELY

- "I was working with a PR agency that was representing a highway logistics company. I knew the agency was interested in getting favorable coverage for their client, but I was impressed that they were able to suggest a variety of possible story ideas (including some that didn't pertain very much to their client). I ended up working with the agency on a story about the day-to-day activities of trucking firms moving goods along this highway corridor. The PR agency was very helpful, and once I started digging into the story, I found that their client was a perfect fit for the article." – *Editor, real estate development publisher*

- "One software company pitched me on a product that I didn't think was part of my coverage area. However, they were able to relate it to subjects that I do cover and made me see that it was relevant to my beat, even though people didn't think of it that way. This made it both interesting and newsworthy. They also provided customer references: a huge plus." – *Editor, IT and data management Website*

- "An email came about the proliferation of serialized dramas during the upcoming TV season, offering an interview with an analyst who believed these shows were going to cannibalize one another. As it turned out, I was already working on a story about this subject, and the woman making the pitch got information to me quickly and got me on the phone with the analyst with great speed." – *Reporter, major daily newspaper in Southern California*

RESPECT JOURNALISTS' PROFESSIONALISM

- "A local hospital PR guy who has a background in radio does a great job of pitching story ideas and then making doctors and others available for us to interview. I think it helps when a PR person has some media experience. Conversely, we recently had a PR person deliver homogenized quotes from some questions a reporter posed as possible interview questions. We were encouraged to use any of the quotes and attribute them to any of the people she talked with. That was completely unacceptable. And unethical. We need PR people to help us make the contacts for the story, not do the reporting for us." – *Reporter, daily newspaper in mid-size metro market*

- "From a non-profit that helps undeveloped communities abroad develop water districts. Spoke to me like a journalist, with compelling numbers, people, and why anyone would give a flying @#$!" - *Editor, major consumer finance Website*

- "Just say what you've got and why it's news. Also, know something about the publication and the reporter. Don't pitch trade press stories to newspapers, for example." – *Reporter, Washington, DC political trade magazine*

POLITE PERSISTENCE CAN BE EFFECTIVE

- "A really good PR exec sent me a pitch for a case study with all of the important info early on the e-mail and then followed that (in the same e-mail) with a longer, more formal pitch." – *Business management publisher*

- "I received a pitch for an interview with a Sun health-IT executive that was straight to the point, quickly told me what product news Sun had to convey, but also left open the possibility of talking to the executive just to make contact. He was also amenable to any angles I might want to pursue. The interview fit with a larger analysis story I wanted to do, and when I responded that I would like an interview, the PR person then sent me the bio and other information (not before!). The story's approach changed after the interview, based on a number of things the executive said, and the PR person (and the executive) was completely willing to roll with that, even though it meant the focus became more on a Sun customer than on Sun itself." – *Editor, IT publisher and Website*

- "Regular email updates…made me feel like an insider on [a client's] progress." – *Reporter, entertainment trade industry Website*

- "Send an email, then call ten minutes later to see if we got it. Don't send a release last week, then call this week about something that is happening next month. Make it timely. Also, remember assignment editors only have about one minute per phone call." – *Producer, local affiliate of CBS TV*

THE COMPLETE PACKAGE

Finally, here's an anecdote from a reporter at a major metropolitan daily newspaper that sums up what I would call the complete package pitching effort. Notice how in this example, the person making the pitch already had established a relationship with the columnist. Using this relationship, she asked in advance about sending a pitch. Then she sent the pitch and followed up with additional information, when requested. After the article was published, she sent a short thank you note and indicated an interest in continuing to work with the columnist.

> *"Recently, I received a request for coverage from a local history organization that was having a fund-raising auction. One of the officers, whom I already knew, sent me a personal email asking if I could announce the event in my column. She emailed me three weeks before the event, indicated that she knew how the column was structured by suggesting where and when the item could run, gave me the basic facts on the auction and what the proceeds would be used for, put in a hyperlink to the page on the Web site where there were details about the auction, and offered to send high-resolution photos of some of the more interesting antiques for sale. When I asked for the photos, I received them within 24 hours, which was fine, since it was not a daily deadline situation.*

The day after the item ran, she sent a nice email thanking me for featuring their event, noting that she would be happy to help if I ever needed information for my column on the area her organization represents. It's a pleasure to work with this organization, and I hope to interact with them in the future."

Conclusion

Each interaction with a journalist is unique. Sometimes you and your pitch will click with the journalist, and sometimes you won't. You can increase your odds significantly if you do things right. As the examples in this chapter reveal, journalists quickly focus on whether a pitch offers an angle that relates to their readers. Within a minute or less, they will decide if your idea is worth pursuing. And if they do want to follow up for an interview, they expect to receive your attention and commitment in return. Remember, you contacted them first and asked for their time to consider your pitch.

Yet, journalists are not expecting you to do their jobs for them. To the contrary, if they sense that you are encroaching on their turf, they will react negatively. Journalists want the information you can provide, but they (and their editors) retain control over the use of that information and its distribution to their audience. Your goal is to demonstrate that your ideas and your resources will help them do their jobs; then you stand a good chance of having your pitch evolve into a news or feature article.

CHAPTER 8

The Worst of Pitching

W hat do these four things have in common?
  Shotguns
  Fishing
  Hype
  Gunk

These are the four most common traits of bad pitching—as identified by journalists who took our survey. As you will see in the comments compiled below, pitchers are too often guilty of distributing information that frustrates and annoys journalists. Poor pitches propose topics that are not covered by the media outlets they are contacting, and they are poorly written and/or much too long. They lack newsworthy information, or they focus solely on the pitcher rather than the benefits to the audience. The worst offenders violate the boundaries between journalism and advertising or advocacy, and they will poison a relationship with the media.

As the following comments indicate, professionals, as well as the publicists who serve them, make these mistakes. This is your chance to learn how to avoid them.

SHOTGUNS

Distribute the same pitch to masses of reporters – the shotgun approach is a common mistake. The idea (and it has reached epidemic proportions in the email era) is that a lot of random activity is sure to generate some attention. The shot-gunner thinks that if 300 reporters see the pitch, a few are surely going to use it. The shot-gunner could not be more wrong.

I am an advocate of the sniper rifle approach to pitching. Select a couple of reporters in different forms of media, and offer your story as an exclusive. Make them aware that you will not shop the pitch around to other journalists until they have decided whether or not to use it. You will earn their respect, regardless of their decision to pick up on a particular idea that you have presented.

FISHING

If you have ever been deep-sea fishing, you probably have seen trawlers with ten different lines in the water at once. They hope that by having a lot of lines out there, something will bite. In pitching, the trawler equivalent is sending many story ideas to the same journalist in rapid succession, hoping that one idea will have the right appeal.

PR people and professionals who trawl don't land the big catch. Chances are they will annoy the heck out of the journalists they are trying to attract. My business targets its pitches and keeps track of what pitches were distributed to whom, and when. We make sure we are not annoying our targets with too much information and too many scattered ideas. Reporters receive hundreds of emails and faxes every week with different pitches and ideas. The more you send, the more you add to the chaos.

HYPE

Empty promises are a serious breach of trust and respect. Think back to the bombastic pronouncements of boxing promoter Don King whenever Mike Tyson would fight in the 1990s. Every fight was going to be the start of the greatest career comeback in boxing history. But when the fight actually took place, each person who spent $99 on the Pay-Per-View channel was disappointed. The fights were sluggish and dull. Sometimes Tyson knocked out an overmatched foe in less than a round, and other times he was outclassed within minutes.

Don't be the Don King of your industry. If you talk glowingly of a story idea, an expert, service, or product, be sure you can back up the hype. Otherwise, you will be the one knocked out on the canvas!

GUNK

"Cut to the chase" is one of the mantras I repeat to my employees and my clients. When people communicate with you, you naturally prefer them to be short and to the point. Journalists are the same way.

People tend to talk or write too much, especially in the financial services industry where I spend the majority of my consulting time. Personal finance matters are complex, and the investment issues that are part of the equation are very complicated. Sometimes my clients feel that they need to say more, and more, and more. They argue with me that they are giving the complete picture. I have to remind them that the reporters and producers are not in a position to present the complete picture to their audiences, especially based on a single pitch.

Sometimes my clients make a very valid point that their comments must be accompanied by a series of legal disclaimers that are required by federal and/or state law. They blame disclaimers for their wordiness. However, I remind them that they are working with professionals. They can take a moment to remind the reporter that their comments are accompanied by legal disclaimers, and then should provide the disclaimers. But they should not interrupt their actual message in a pitch or an interview to go over the details of the disclaimers. They will quickly lose the attention of the journalist.

A pitch may have merit and may apply to the outlet in question, but if a reporter has to dig through the information to identify the hook or angle, he or she will move on to something else. Be respectful of reporters' time, and they will be respectful of the time you took to prepare and send the pitch.

Worst Pitches

While good pitches are critical to your success, poor execution will undermine an otherwise promising idea. The following comments are from journalists about pitches that have fallen flat and conduct that has annoyed them or wasted their time. We will begin with the greatest offense of all: not taking the time to understand what the reporter and the media outlet are actually interested in covering.

LACK OF UNDERSTANDING OF REPORTER'S BEAT AND MEDIA'S COVERAGE

- "From a PR business that represented a company that made software for institutional investors…. If they had taken the time to read the magazine, they would've realized we are NOT aimed at pension fund managers, and therefore their product had no use for the vast majority of our readers." – *Editor, national personal finance magazine*

- "Nothing is more irritating than when I receive press releases or phone calls from companies outside of what my magazine covers. Know your audience, and don't waste my time! A quick glance at our Web site will give you a good feel for what we cover." - *Reporter, military affairs publisher*

- "Pitches that have nothing to do with what I cover. I receive dozens of them every day. I especially don't like cold calls that have nothing to do with what I cover and never-ending follow-ups asking if I've received the pitch. If it's something I'm interested in, I'll keep it in my background files and I'll call when I'm working on that topic." – *Editor, national personal finance magazine*

- "Tech story…not on my beat… that's basically a product pitch. I get lots of those." – *Producer, cable TV and Web network*

- "There is a PR person for a major insurance brokerage firm who, even after I explained to her the nature of my beat and the audience, continues to contact me about unrelated stories.

In particular, when I was writing on the impact of the HIPAA privacy regulations on employers, she wanted to pitch a story on the impact it would have on health plans and providers—not our audience." – *Editor, insurance trade publisher*

- "I get pitched all the time from flaks who clearly don't know our publication. They offer stories that would never appear in our paper. It is a waste of time for everyone." – *Reporter, national business daily*

- "I hate it when a PR rep calls and has clearly never looked at my magazine. They don't know what kind of editorial I run or what monthly features we have." – *Editor, regional lifestyle magazine*

- "I receive too many blind email attachments from publicists who appear not research the type of writing I usually do. This wastes time." – *Book reviewer, specializing in African-American market*

- "[A recent bad pitch] was for a service of interest to institutional managers (not my readership), and it had so many attachments (8 megabytes) it shut down my computer." – *Reporter, financial industry trade publication*

- "I received some sort of muscle-mass building powder in a mail as a test product, I guess. The release talked about the product but didn't really pitch it or seem to know exactly what we write about (we don't do product reviews). This was the first I had heard of it. I would have preferred an email introduction from the person to see if we covered things like this, and if I would be interested in receiving a test sample, rather than just automatically sending it." – *Reporter, national consumer news wire service*

- "If I see that the subject is not pertinent to my area of interest, which is local and Texas history, I tend to trash or delete these without reading. I also am unlikely to bother to read anything else sent to me by a PR firm that does this." – *Reporter, major metro daily newspaper*

GEOGRAPHIC STUPIDITY

- "A PR professional called to pitch me a story about restaurants in Texas. Not a subject I cover, and it was the wrong state."
  – Reporter, major metro area daily newspaper

- "Started out by not stating in email what the release was about, then went on to describe the interest to my community, though it was about someone from out-of-state who had no connection to local community. It showed they did not know my readers, coverage area, or publication day, etc. The message was very commercial…from a clothing company … and said that my community needs the information to be ready for winter. 'Needs to know!' Give me a break—the fashions were for snow attire, and we are in Southern California!" *– Feature writer, Southern California lifestyle magazine and Web site*

- "Be sure you have checked all the details. Someone in Columbus, Ga., doesn't want to waste time with a story pitch from the capital of Ohio (which is also Columbus). That's happened a few times."
  – News reporter, mid-size metro daily newspaper

POOR WRITING

- "The important information such as who, what, where, when, and why are scattered and buried within text that is meaningless to me. I haven't time to wade through the gunk." *– Reporter, financial trade press magazine*

- "A poorly written pitch that I received came by email about a coming fundraiser. It included very few details, spelling mistakes, and was very demanding." *– Reporter, Western Canada daily newspaper*

- "Vague recollection of one that used abbreviated text-message style language. Seemed unprofessional. Typos also typical, but the worst in general are those with wrong information, including misspelled names." *– Reporter, mid-size metro daily newspaper*

- "Many of them are rife with misspellings and grammatical errors…and too broad, with no understanding of our newsletter's focus or timing needs." – *Editor, entertainment industry magazine*

- "Often, I receive pitches where the relevant info is buried in the story. I have to search for the date/time/location the story is occurring, and have to search for the contact name and number of the publicist." – *Reporter, Fox TV affiliate*

- "Too many pitches are poorly written and presented. They pitch us for stories we don't cover, pitch us for stories that are outside of our local area (which only wastes our time and theirs), and call us on Thursdays and Fridays when we're on deadline for Monday's paper." – *Editor, chain of national business weeklies*

LACK OF NEWS ANGLE

- "A pitch on information protection was too long, took too long to get to the point, and pitched old news like it was a breaking trend." – *Editor, IT trade Web site*

- "People call every day wanting us to do stories about their business, just because it's their business. The 'pitch' is often the same one they should be giving to prospective customers, not the media." – *Producer, TV affiliate of national network*

- "Here is an example of a pitch that is way too general. On just this one issue, I got about 20 others like it." – *Reporter, national consumer publication*

> *President George Bush signed the Pension Protection Act of 2006. The Pension Protection Act Contains Provisions To Help American Workers Who Save For Retirement Through Defined Contribution Plans, Like IRAs And 401(k)s, including automatic enrollment in 401(k) retirement savings programs. This is the most radical change for the most commonly used retirement saving program since it has overtaken the defined pension plans that appear to be going the way of the dinosaur.*

Sandy Stone (name changed), *who manages Benefit Interest* (company name changed), *a 401(k) provider, is a superb spokesperson on how this change will affect businesses who offer 401(k) plans and for the participants of those plans. Sandy helped launch Benefit Interest in 1992 and has been in the employee benefits arena since 1988, so she knows her business...*

OVERLY AGGRESSIVE PRODUCT OR PEOPLE PROMOTION

- "Story ideas that are clearly promoting a certain product or company." – *Editor, consumer lifestyle publication*

- "The worst is a series of pitches I receive from different people at the same PR firm who are all trying to set up interviews with the same CEO. These pitches come once or twice a week, and the underlying subject is always different. I think they're trying to make me think this executive is an expert on everything, but my takeaway is that he's just trying to get in the press." – *Financial news wire service*

- "While researching a story about Nebraska, I telephoned a PR guy representing a prominent Omaha lawyer. I mentioned that I wanted to interview the lawyer as an expert for my Nebraska story, but the PR guy immediately started maneuvering and conniving to get an additional profile feature written on his client. I found his style to be brutish and bullying; he was asking me to do a story I had not been assigned. It was simply beyond my power to grant his request, and as a result he started micromanaging access to his client. I didn't write the profile piece, though I was finally able to get an interview with his client for the larger story at hand." – *Reporter, national construction and development publisher*

- "Actually, the worst pitches I've received read more like fishing expeditions. I had a company routinely email me and ask me what my plans were for stories based on what they read in my editorial calendar. Don't ask me what I want to write: Pitch me a story that will make me want to write about your client!" – *Reporter, federal regulatory newsletter*

EXCESSIVE FOCUS ON PITCHER, NOT ON TOPIC

- "The worst go on and on about some person's credentials. I routinely hear from someone who is pitching books and goes on and on about everything the author ever did or said and everyone he ever spoke to. I don't have time for that." – *Reporter, mid-size metro daily newspaper*

- "They all sound like corporate advertisements that make the corporate executives sound nice, but do nothing to present a news story." – *Reporter, major metro area daily newspaper*

- "When I was a newspaper reporter, I would routinely get calls from local PR people and business owners asking for a 'write up' of their company or product." – *Freelance business writer*

- "Without mentioning the company, it was from a national drug store chain. The idea it was trying to push was to provide information about heat and hot-weather injuries, but was written with weak grammar and seemed to be a giant free commercial for the company. Interestingly enough, they never ran [an advertising] schedule on the station. They were obviously trying to get on the air free." – *Producer, ABC local affiliate*

LACK OF RESPECT FOR A REPORTER'S TIME

- "Long, wordy emails or phone calls that don't get to the point." – *Producer, CBS News affiliate*

- "I had a release that was at least two pages in length. There was no information about what was going on, just a slew of plugs for different companies. The PR rep called when she had sent the release and then called every day to see if I had run the release in the paper." – *Reporter, mid-size metro daily newspaper*

"PR people who call at deadline and won't get off the phone, or demand my promise that a story will be written." – *Reporter, national business news wire service*

LACK OF ORGANIZATION

"One company had three different reps pitch me three different ways...each of whom seemed unaware that the others were pitching me. I said no every time. If you're going to try to convince me, at least be organized." – *Editor, IT trade journal, specializing in product reviews*

INSUFFICIENT INFORMATION

"It's important to me to receive sufficient detail to be able to make a decision on the pitch without having to chase down the writer with a phone call. Many of the pitch letters/press releases I receive come from volunteers who are not used to writing; they are apt to leave out something major, such as the date or address of an event. 'Detailed' doesn't have to mean 'long.' A rambling, multi-page pitch may have nuggets of useful information buried in disorganized verbiage." – *Reporter, major metro daily newspaper*

"Recently, my editor requested that a company send me a promotional copy of the new Jerry Lee Lewis album for review. When the bare-bones promo copy arrived in its broken jewel case, it included no production notes, no session details, and no back story about the troubles this project had finding a label. All of this is important to a review of the disc and adds to Jerry Lee Lewis's legend. I had to ask for the information, and the company in question simply didn't have the information." – *Reviewer, music industry press*

"A property appraiser called, urging me to encourage readers to attend city budget public hearings to encourage city council to hold down taxes. The appraiser didn't seem to understand that public input at this stage was a last-ditch effort, and was overly optimistic. He provided no information on the impact of the proposed budget on local residents, nor suggested specific people to call." – *Business reporter, mid-size metro daily newspaper*

- "On the medical science front, most pitches are too technical and require at least one or two phone calls to get a complete explanation in layman's terms." – *Freelance medical science reporter and producer*

LACK OF EXCLUSIVITY

- "I don't want to receive broadcast faxes or emails sent to all columnists at every newspaper." – *Reporter, major metro daily newspaper*

- "A shotgun pitch, sent to 'undisclosed recipients,' painted an advertorial picture of the company and its product—but with no info on users, value, innovation in the market, issues addressed, nor problems perceived." – *Editor, photography and audio-visual trade publication*

- "Numerous times lately I've received pitches that say 'Dear,' without my name inserted, or pitches to 'Dear Reporter' or 'Dear Journalist,' or that have no signature at the bottom or that are clearly in some other draft state. I automatically delete those, figuring that if the PR person won't take the time to personalize the pitch, I'm not even going to bother to read what they've sent me." – *Reporter, IT industry magazine and Web publisher*

- "One woman insists on sending me pitches, but in the email address it is addressed to someone else. I don't know how this happens. When I told her about it, she pretty much said I was wrong." – *Reporter, IT publisher*

HYPE AND EXAGGERATION

- "Most [bad pitches] concern obscure, up-and-coming artists that nobody knows and nobody cares about. The content is trivial, and the publicist makes it sound as if it were a life-changing event." – *Freelance music and arts reviewer*

➤ "Any time a PR person pitches a client with certain story and/or products that, when you get to the interview, simply don't exist." – *Producer, local NBC-TV affiliate*

➤ "Oh, just about every one trying to get me to interview the 3rd- or 4th- or 5th-billed star on a TV show, when I've done a story like that for my newspaper in, well, never." – *Entertainment and features reporter, major metro daily newspaper*

➤ "People pitching things like has-been stars who want to talk about heart-smart cooking. If it doesn't suit my show, I don't want it." – *Producer, feature stories, national networks*

LACK OF AVAILABILITY FOR FOLLOW-UP

➤ "Too many publicists are out of the office the day before an event. Don't take the day off on a day that people need to get in touch with you." – *Reporter, Fox TV affiliate*

POOR PHONE MESSAGE ETIQUETTE

➤ "The worst are voicemail pitches in which someone calls and spends more than two minutes explaining something (that I often already know about) before leaving a phone number, which is usually only given once and then given so quickly that I have to listen to the message again to get the call-back number correct. And what happened to diction on the phone?" - *Reporter, mid-size metro daily newspaper*

IRRELEVANT INFORMATION

➤ "[One PR person who contacts me regularly] must have a desire to be a fiction writer. Every pitch comes with at least a 200-word reference to something completely unrelated, in an effort to entice, I guess. One intro waxed lyrical about her opinion of a cult horror hit and why it would do well at the box office. The pitch was for a new technology." – *Reporter, IT trade press*

INSULTS

- "I got an email from an industry front group once that had the subject line, 'The story the media won't report,' or something like that. That's rude. Also, I've had PR people I didn't know send me stories published by our competition with notes along the lines of, 'You might want to cover this, too.' That is VERY aggravating."
  – Political reporter, Washington, DC

Conclusion

Media professionals have a difficult job. They must master many topics, often in rapid succession or even simultaneously. They face unforgiving deadlines, often on a daily basis. Their competition is relentless, and it is proliferating in this era of easy online news distribution. Journalists' mistakes are made public instantly, and the whole world is eager to pounce on those mistakes.

Don't make journalists' jobs more difficult. When you send a pitch, make sure you are targeting the right journalist, or at least the right publication. Your pitch should be precise, concise, and to the point. Your pitch must have news value, and you should make sure not to over-hype its importance. If you say that you or other experts will be available for interviews, make sure you do respond promptly to the inquiry and return calls by deadline. When being interviewed, tell the truth. Treat members of the media with respect, and you will be treated with respect in return.

PRinciples of Pitching

I n September 2007, my wife, Wendy and I became first-time parents. Although we were scared to death, nothing could make us any happier or more excited, too. As we anticipated the challenges of parenthood, we talked about what is necessary to raise a child in this world, and how we can help her develop into a healthy, productive member of society. We agree that children need to be raised on principles and with some structure. Without either, children can become lost and disoriented.

Developing a positive PR approach and fostering relationships with the media is like raising a child. You need to have a sound structure and a clear set of principles. I call these the PRinciples of PR. By embracing these principles every day, you will stay focused on what really matters. You will get your brand message out to the right people, at the right time, and in the right format. You will present yourself as knowledgeable and current in your profession, and attuned to the needs of customers and prospects. You will build your network of contacts and supporters. And you will probably learn a few things from people you talk with, giving you ideas about how to improve your company.

The PRinciples of PR:

PRactitioner	PResentation
PRinciples	PRemeditate
PRincipals	PRecise
PRess release	PRompt
PRepare	PRetend
PRocess	PRactice
PResume	PRomote
PRudent	PRosper

PRACTITIONER

Effective media relations are built on rapport with journalists, editors, producers, and everyone else involved in the creation and dissemination of news and features. This is why the commitment of the PRactitioner—that's you—is so important.

To become a trusted resource for the media, you must know what your strengths are (your brand) and how you want to portray them to the public. You must define your target media market and reach out to its individual members. You must share information with the media that is timely, complete, and accurate. You must

Don't Be a Crash Test Dummy

Wrong, silly, or offensive statements can haunt a company for years. Political gaffes are the most prominent examples of what we call Crash Test Dummies, but they occur all the time in the business environment, too. This problem is even greater now than ever before, as blogs, YouTube, and other electronic media make it simple for mistakes to be widely shared.

In hindsight, these Crash Test Dummy statements are funny. But you can be sure that they caused endless problems at the time.

"I invented the Internet." – *Former VP Al Gore*

"If you take out the killings, Washington, D.C., actually has a very low crime rate." – *Former D.C. Mayor Marion Barry*

"I can't believe we are going to let a majority of the people decide what is best for this state." – *U.S. Rep. John Travis (Louisiana)*

"The President has kept all of the promises he intended to keep."
– *George Stephanopolous, spokesman for former President Bill Clinton*

demonstrate expertise and credibility within your field. Bottom line: Great pitching begins with you.

PRINCIPLES

Top professionals in any industry abide by important principles in operating their businesses and conducting their lives. Principles such as honesty, integrity, and fulfilling promises are as important in developing good relationships with the press as they are in delivering superior services to customers and clients.

Surely, you operate your business according to strong principles, and you expect your staff to uphold these standards, too. Your principles are your core messages; they represent what you stand for in your business. You should be able to articulate these quickly and clearly to any audience—a client, a prospect, a new employee, a vendor, and the media.

You must be able to tie these principles to specific activities of your firm and explain how you demonstrate them in the marketplace every day. Your principles are at once central to your core, but also timeless standards that are bigger than your company.

PRINCIPALS

Having a great brand, a great message, and great principles are not enough to ensure success with the media. You also must be attentive to who is actually representing your company in public – whether at an industry conference, a public hearing, or to the media. This is why your principals are so important.

Make sure that the people from your organization who speak with the media are qualified to do so and that they fully understand the brand and your principles. An inaccurate statement or a poorly timed joke can undermine years of effort to project a certain image.

PRESS RELEASE

In Chapter 4, we explored in detail how a press release differs from a pitch. If you can grasp the difference and use each for the appropriate purpose, you will be ahead of most of your competition. The fact is that most business executives in most companies simply don't know the difference. Sadly, many account managers and copywriters at PR firms don't know the difference either.

A press release typically contains general information, and it is not designed to appeal to one publication or media outlet. It might announce that your firm has entered a new line of business or purchased a competitor. It might announce the promotion of an executive. It might announce the completion of a project, such as a facility expansion or a property development. A press release serves the purpose of keeping your company in the mind of the media, but it does not necessarily suggest a specific story.

In contrast, a pitch is the suggestion of a specific story idea to a specific media outlet. It has been carefully developed to appeal to an audience that is served by a particular media outlet (and often, a specific member of the media).

Whether developing a press release or a pitch, you must pay attention to making the information newsworthy for the audience you are trying to reach. Ask yourself these questions.

- *Is the information timely?* As the survey data in Chapter 6 and the anecdotes in Chapters 7 and 8 emphasized, you must know the deadlines. A daily newspaper will not find information that is a month old to be valuable, but a quarterly newsletter might.

- *Is the information unusual or controversial or entertaining?* Publications need to capture and hold their readers' attention. Reporters, editors, and producers always are seeking to highlight the interesting angle. Your job is to help them quickly identify that angle.

➤ *Is the information relevant to a majority of the audience?* All media outlets have audiences that share certain traits. A local TV news telecast audience lives in the same geographic region. Professional journal readers share professional and academic interests. Web site visitors share an interest in that topic. Make sure that you target your information at a large segment of that audience; you stand a better chance of having the public contact your company (or your client's).

PRESENTATION – PITCH STRUCTURE

In developing a pitch, the structure can be as important as the content of your idea. The people in the media are very busy, and they need to find out what you are saying as quickly as possible. The survey results highlight what happens when you send a pitch to the wrong publication: Reporters ignore you because you have not bothered to learn what topics matter to them.

Here are some basic rules to ensure that your written pitch is presented clearly and efficiently.

➤ Keep it short and to the point
➤ State your assertion in the first paragraph. Make sure it has a news "hook"
➤ Limit the pitch to four paragraphs (plus contact information at the end)
➤ Use bullet points
➤ Find facts and statistics to back up the assertion
➤ Provide thorough contact information

For telephone pitches, the same principles apply. Be polite and get right to your point. Indicate why you think the idea is timely and relevant to the media outlet you are contacting. Offer to provide backup information by email, so that the reporter can review it at a convenient time. Articulate contact information clearly on all voicemail messages.

In addition to structuring the pitch properly, you need to distribute it properly. This means that you should investigate how your target media member wishes to receive information—electronically, by fax, by phone, etc.—and at which time of the week and the day. You also need to know the editorial cycle of the publication or electronic media, so that you are making contact with sufficient time for the editor to respond.

One more item of insider advice. It is appropriate to leave a short phone message to alert a reporter that you will be sending an email pitch about a particular topic. But if you leave the pre-pitch phone message, don't also leave a follow-up call to ask if the pitch was received. At that point, you are becoming a nuisance. Reporters will contact you if they are interested.

PREPARE AND PREMEDITATE

In all walks of life, preparation leads to success. Effective pitching requires premediation and preparation long before you are ready to write your first pitch. Begin your outreach effort by fine-tuning

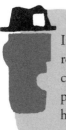

If you are a financial advisor, you might choose to pitch an idea related to a specific savings program that you recommend for your clients. For example, if you are an expert on college savings plans, pitch an article about the high cost of colleges in your area, and how long-term savings plans can reduce the financial bite on a typical family.

For your pitch, prepare real-life case histories that show how a family can save for college. Use real numbers for current college costs and projected cost increases. Compare those costs to the typical median wage in your area. Be as specific as possible. If possible, pre-arrange with a client family that they will be available to discuss their experiences—while guaranteeing to them that the necessary confidentiality will be preserved.

your own brand definition and selling points. Define clearly what you can do best for your customers and prospects. From that point, you build your pitching strategy—linked to both your unique skills, as well as to issues that matter to the target audience.

With premediation, you have defined what you are and where you want to be. You are prepared to share your information with the media through ideas they can sink their journalistic teeth into.

Next, you have to follow up by delivering on your promise. Again, you have to be prepared. Prior to sending your pitch, you should carefully examine the various angles to the story you are pitching, and prepare your key facts and major themes. Have your data handy.

PROCESS AND PROMPTNESS

No two journalists are exactly alike with regards to how they like to communicate with sources and PR representatives. Although our survey shows that most prefer email today, you still will benefit by taking the time to understand the process that each reporter prefers.

Try to determine the reporter's preferences for:

- Time of day
- Method of communication
- Deadlines
- Beats
- Follow-up process

How do you figure that out? You ask. Most journalists are quite willing to tell you how they like to be contacted and which topics are their primary beats. They understand that it is in their best interests to receive high-quality information and timely ideas from reputable sources. It is also in their best interests to make sure you know what format is most convenient for them.

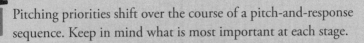

Pitching priorities shift over the course of a pitch-and-response sequence. Keep in mind what is most important at each stage.

Initially, the most important part of the pitch process is presenting an idea that is relevant to the journalist's audience of readers, listeners or viewers. As we saw in the survey, reporters become annoyed when they receive pitches that demonstrate the pitcher has not learned about the coverage of the publication. Journalists dislike when the pitch is focused on the pitcher, rather than the media's audience.

Later, after a pitch has been made, the emphasis shifts to responding to the journalist's inquiry. If a reporter has returned the contact, you cannot focus on your message as much as you need to respond to the questions that the reporter has raised. You can make your points, too, but you need to help reporters complete their assignments, regardless of whether you would emphasize the same details. If the questions are outside of your expertise, admit it.

As you work with the reporter, deadlines are all-important. When reporters say they have a deadline, they really mean it—especially in today's fast-paced media world. If you meet a deadline, you will solidify a relationship for the long-term. If you miss a deadline, you will potentially ruin a contact forever.

It cannot be emphasized enough that you need to respect a reporter's need for a prompt response. You need to meet any commitment you make. So if you say you will return a call by noon, you need to return the call by noon.

Finally, after an article has been published, conduct a little follow-up with the reporter by email or phone. Extend your appreciation of the contact and coverage, and, if appropriate, suggest additional avenues of inquiry for a future article.

PRESUME

Do not presume anything when talking with a journalist. If you expect a reporter to cover your story or quote you because you did an interview, you may be disappointed. Many restrictions and limitations are placed on reporters. Sometimes they are focused on a particular angle in a story, in which you are only a minor player. Sometimes their editor demands wholesale changes. Sometimes a publication runs out of editorial space, or a TV or radio program runs out of airtime. Just because you take the time for them does not mean you will be covered.

Also, do not presume that what you said will be used in the way that you prefer. Journalists make their own judgments about how an article or news telecast will be most valuable to their audience. They have an intimate understanding of their audience's interests, level of sophistication, prior knowledge of a subject, and so on. Their knowledge of their audience's demographics, income and wealth levels, and other factors also affect how they conduct their reporting.

So when journalists cover an issue, they are doing it in the way that they believe will be most meaningful—even if you do feel that the emphasis should be elsewhere. You can offer your input on other factors that the journalist should include in an article, but you will not be able to dictate how the article is written.

Bottom Line: Each interview that you do builds credibility and rapport with the media. You are showing your expertise and demonstrating your willingness to help. In the big picture, getting quoted in a specific story is less important than having the long-term relationship that will yield more opportunities and a chance to have deeper conversations with the media.

One of my clients was eager to be interviewed by any of the major personal finance publications (Kiplinger's, Money, etc.). After several months of diligent effort, he received a call about which investment strategies would be "hot" in the next year. He spent about 15 minutes on the phone, explaining why he believed that energy was the place to invest, and how this meshed with his underlying investment philosophy.

When the issue of the magazine came out a month later, the advisor was not quoted. He was furious. "Why did I waste my time with that reporter?" he asked me.

I explained that probably an editor higher in the chain made some cuts in the article, and his comments were eliminated. I counseled my client to remain patient.

Sure enough, six months later we saw a golden opportunity. The energy sector that my client recommended had done very well since the interview with the reporter. So we wrote a story pitch with the title: "Why energy has been booming—and why it will continue."

My client received a call from the same reporter, and he was a major source in a feature article.

PRECISION

Readers rely upon reporters for accurate and unbiased information, and they take their roles seriously. If you do anything that undermines the credibility of a reporter, you have lost that resource permanently.

Do not twist the truth in a pitch or an interview. Be precise and accurate. Otherwise, you will quickly doom your chance to ever work with that reporter or media outlet again.

Also, do not misrepresent your business expertise. If you are an attorney who does not know about real estate law, do not send a story pitch about real estate. Your ignorance will be exposed when the reporter calls you with detailed questions.

Even if you could "fake" your way through an interview and get quoted, how would it help your business? Do you really want prospects calling you to analyze real estate deals if you don't know what you are doing?

Here are some tips:

- Conduct fact-checking before distributing information to the media

- Cite independent sources of information

- If you are including anecdotes about real people, find out in advance if they are willing to speak to the media

- Never lie

- If you are not an expert, suggest colleagues who are more knowledgeable

- If the reporter raises issues that disagree with your perspective, acknowledge the differences, and explain your side of the story. Do not attack

PRUDENCE

Before you pitch a story, think carefully about who is receiving the idea. We have said it before, but we will say it again: Make sure you know what a reporter's beat is and whether or not he or she covers that topic. If you send information to the wrong reporter, you will be wasting everyone's time (including yours), and you might undermine the credibility you have been working hard to achieve.

Broadly speaking, there are two types of media professionals today. Some work for general interest outlets, such as daily metropolitan area newspapers or television stations. Others work for specialty publications, such as professional magazines, journals, or Web sites; these are often known as the "trade press."

The sophistication level of the audience and the journalist varies greatly between these two categories. Before contacting a reporter, you should be clear about which type of audience the medium is serving.

If you are seeking to reach a general consumer audience, then the reporter is likely to be a generalist, too with numerous beats, or a single beat that is very broad. The reporter probably has to write about many different topics, but only at a moderate level of depth.

A single reporter might be responsible for all news from the state capital, for example. It is unrealistic to expect that reporter to know many specific details about the wetlands initiative in your state that your environmental organization is pitching. You will need to be prepared to do some education on the issue, perhaps by offering to send background materials after your initial pitch. You should make sure that someone from your organization can spend time on the phone getting the reporter "up to speed" on the issue. The lead time for the reporter to produce an article could be significant, too, as the reporter might want to contact several other people to verify the claims that you are making and to get differing viewpoints.

On the other hand, if you are contacting a reporter at a trade publication in your industry, the interaction could be very different. Most likely, an experienced reporter already understands the technical, business, and regulatory aspects of your issue—to some degree. The reporter probably already knows people on both sides of the issue, if it's controversial. For this reporter, you can skip the basic information and get right to the point. You will need to be prepared to provide much more sophisticated data and analysis to support your ideas, instead of simpler background material. You might need to call in your best technical or legal experts to respond to some issues that the reporter has raised.

As noted elsewhere, too, prudence also comes from pitching ideas that truly are in your area of expertise. You are setting yourself up for failure or embarrassment if you present yourself incorrectly. A journalist might be interested in your pitch, but when he or she interviews you, the truth will emerge. You will not be able to answer sophisticated questions, and the reporter will not use the general or vague information that you provide. Nothing will have been accomplished.

PRACTICE

Rather than singing the latest Brittany Spears or U2 song in the shower or in your car, try practicing for that big interview you have coming up on TV or in your local newspaper. You have always heard, "practice makes perfect." Well, it does; rehearsing before an interview will help you phrase your message and anticipate the dialogue of the interview.

Practice how you would respond to specific questions, and anticipate potential follow-up questions to your answers. It might be effective to write notes for your answers (after you get out of the shower!), so that you will not forget to mention all of the major points.

If other people in your firm are qualified to respond to questions from the media, make sure that they have been copied on your pitch and understand that they might be contacted. Ensure that each of your principals shares the same data and information. You need to present a consistent message to the media, both about your firm's brand and also about the specific issues raised by your pitch.

Tip: Practice out loud. How you respond to questions when you vocalize is a lot different than saying it in your head.

PROMOTE

Do not assume that your clients and prospects have seen your media coverage. To get the most out of your coverage, you need to share it. If you are quoted in the newspaper or will be on TV or radio, send a quick email with a link to your client database. Most TV and radio outlets archive their work, so you can even send the link after the show has aired. Send another reminder in your company's newsletter, which will keep your appearance alive for several months.

PROSPER

You can prosper with the media if you truly understand the rules of engagement. We have addressed these several times in the book, but a concise listing here is helpful to review.

- Be available to the media
- Suggest relevant and timely ideas
- Be patient—first efforts often are not rewarded
- Be accurate and truthful
- Honor deadlines
- Be polite and professional. Respect journalists' professionalism

Journalists are professionals, and they have difficult jobs. They are seeking to work with people who can help them do their jobs better—present interesting, useful information to their audience. By helping them do their jobs, you will gain their trust and their support. You will serve your own interests, and just as importantly, the interests of the public that the journalists serve.

Tip: Send a thank you note. If you are quoted after an interview, take a minute to send a very short thank you note to the reporter by e-mail. Express your appreciation for the opportunity to share information, and add that you are willing to be contacted again. This short communication will remind the reporter that you are staying on top of the topics that he or she covers.

Conclusion

Winning pitching and effective PR come from a thoughtful, dedicated approach to defining your brand, targeting the correct members of the media, and making a commitment to providing valuable information on a consistent basis.

I have found that it is helpful to think about the elements of successful pitching and public relations as being built on a series of core PRinciples. These tried-and-true practices have worked for thousands of PR professionals and their clients. They can work for you, too.

Pitch Samples

T he following are examples of pitches we have seen first-hand at Perception, Inc. that fit the model of effective pitches. They easily met one or more of the newsworthiness criteria and were developed in a way that caught the attention of the journalists.

Client: Barry Glassman, CFP® of Cassaday & Company

Topic: Surnamed Mutual Funds and Performance

This pitch evolved from a question posed to Barry Glassman, investment advisor, by one of his clients. The deceptively simple question was: "How do mutual funds named after fund managers perform versus other mutual funds?"

Barry didn't know the answer, so he decided to do a little research. He logged on to Morningstar.com and identified 16 surnamed mutual funds. His goal was to see how these 16 funds performed versus the S&P 500 during a bear market and a bull market. After a little time he found some startling results. What follows is the pitch that was distributed to members of the media in June 2003:

> Certified Financial Planner Barry Glassman announced surprising results of recent research in the mutual fund arena. Following up on a perception that mutual funds trading under the manager's name outperformed other funds, he discovered the following:

> ➤ Of the top 500 equity mutual funds ranked by assets under management, 16 funds' names include their manager's name in the title.

> ➤ Of the 16 funds, 100% beat the S&P in 2002, and 15 did so in both 2001 and 2000. Only Marsico Focus fell short.

- This means that 93.7% of the surname funds outperformed the S&P Index as opposed to only vs. 42.2% among a universe of the top 500.

- Turnover within the name-bearing funds was significantly lower, 36% vs. 61% for the top 500 aggregate.

- All but one of the 16 managers has headed up their fund since its inception. In the case of the exception, Chris Davis' father ran the fund before he did.

Glassman also examined expense ratios, P/E, and risk statistics. Clearly, the majorities have positive alphas and low betas, numerical ratings that are used as a gauge of safety vs. risk by fund analysts. The funds also ranged from the very focused (30 holdings for Jensen), to broadly diversified (400+ for Gabelli Asset).

An interesting note was that these funds represented most parts of the equity style box, as well as foreign and real estate.

Glassman speculated as to reasons:

Personal Assets These managers usually have their own assets invested in their funds. According to Davis, the founding family is the largest shareholder in each of their funds - $2.5 billion in total.

Incentives "Who but the owner is in it for the long run?" Glassman said. "Owners have a vested interest in applying prudence and principles with a natural accountability to their shareholders. These managers are not going to fire themselves. Nobody ever points his finger at Mr. Fidelity or puts the blame on Ms. Aim."

Personality Glassman points to the level of confidence someone must possess before he agrees to put his name on the door. Glassman believes "these managers are established, confident individuals."

Maturity and experience Age information was not readily available but may reveal managers who experienced the 70's bear market as well as the 1987 stock market crash kept risk at bay during the most recent three-year bear market.

"Managers matter," claims Glassman. "It's trendy to look at performance and other statistics in evaluating a fund, but we must remember what matters most - the manager who chooses which investments to buy and when to buy them."

What were the results of this terrific pitch?

1. Barry appeared on television's "*Wall Street Week*" with Louis Rukeyser

2. The back page of *Money* magazine published an entire article dedicated to the research

3. *The Washington Post* published an entire page in its business section, which exclaimed, "If he's not famous, he should be!"

4. *Business Week* magazine utilized the research in an article on boutique financial planning firms.

Client: Judson Gee of JHG Financial Advisors

Topic: Solo 401(k) Plans During Layoffs

When we began working with Judson Gee, he made it clear he wanted to be known as the Solo 401(k) guru of Charlotte, NC. Quite a tall order. But before we could begin to position him in this light, we had to find a way to localize the story. Keep this in mind when pitching to local media—always localize the story! Local reporters focus on why an issue, even a national issue, is important to people in their community.

With this idea in mind we set out to work with Judson to identify a way to position Solo 401(k) plans in the Charlotte metro area. One day, Judson called our office with news that a major textile manufacturer in the area that was closing its doors and firing nearly 5,000 employees. His quick thinking and our targeted approach with local media turned Judson into a recognized 401(k) authority almost overnight.

The following pitch that distributed in December 2004:

> Pillowtex Corporation and many other large companies were thriving businesses that employed people throughout the country, Pillowtex with a majority located in the Kannapolis/Concord area, but thanks to rough economic times these companies are now laying off workers, or in the case of Pillowtex, closing altogether because they have not been able to sell linens and towels like they once were able to.
>
> So, what happens now for those workers? Where will they go? What happens to their company-sponsored 401(k) plan and their ability to retire? Although not right for everyone, there is a simple answer to the latter of these questions – a ***Single Owner 401(k) Plan***.
>
> For many workers, finding a new job is not an option. Either they have spent most of their working life at a company such as Pillowtex, or they are unable to find a new job. With the arrival of the Single Owner 401(k), small businesses with no employees that work over 1000 hours annually, including sole proprietorships, partnerships and corporations, incorporated or not, can now provide themselves with a retirement plan similar to the 401(k) plans typically afforded to larger companies.
>
> The Single Owner 401(k) was developed from the Economic Growth and Tax Relief Reconciliation Act of 2001 and permits a small business owner, partners and their spouses, to develop a retirement plan that mimics standard defined contribution plans. In comparison to the typical 401(k), the Single Owner 401(k) is a low cost plan because only one test, the 5500EZ, is needed. However, the combined assets in the plan must exceed $100,000

before administration is performed, usually by the provider. Of course this makes sense because there are typically one to two participants.

- Huge benefits exist for very small businesses when compared to standard 401(k) plans, or comparable retirement plan vehicles. One major difference is the opportunity for higher contributions into the plan. Small business owners can now place 100% of income, or up to $12,000 on a pre-tax basis with additional contributions of 25% of income that could bring the total contribution to $40,000 (cannot exceed the lesser of 100% of payroll or $40,000), plus catch-up contributions for those over age 50. This is exceedingly dissimilar than the 15%, or $12,000 (whichever is less) with a regular 401(k). By increasing the amount of the contribution, small businesses are helping to provide safeguards for future economic stability if a business falls into difficult times.

- Another advantage of the Single Owner 401(k) plan is the ability to consolidate most other types of retirement accounts. For example, if someone is laid off and starts a small business as described above, but has an IRA from their own savings and a 401(k) from a previous employer, he/she can now take the two separate plans and consolidate into one basic account. Increasing the amount of money contributed to the Single Owner 401(k), and increasing the amount consolidated, leaves owners the option of borrowing greater amounts of money from the retirement fund when others sources may not be available, should the need arise.

- The flexible and tax-free loan options also make the Single Owner 401(k) an attractive candidate for small business retirement funds. A small business can borrow directly from their retirement assets – up to 50% of the amount in the fund, or $50,000, whichever is less. Repayment is subject to IRS guidelines. The payment options are offered for two periods, 5 or 10 years, depending on the purpose of the loan. Providers of the new plans are generally well-known name brand investment companies and depending on which provider is used, the interest rate for the loan is fairly low and fixed at the Prime Rate (currently 4.25%) or Prime plus a rate of 1%. The rate is particularly low because the "middle man" is taken out of the equation.

Though there are a few disadvantages to a Single Owner 401(k), the benefits may far outweigh the shortcomings and recently laid off workers and small businesses should consider utilizing the newly offered opportunities that a Single Owner 401(k) can provide.

What were the results of this terrific pitch?

1. Local network affiliates interviewed Judson in front of the manufacturer to discuss the Solo 401(k) as a viable option for laid off workers.

2. *The Charlotte Observer* wrote an article on the issue.

3. *CNBC* picked up on the story and featured Judson on a story about Solo 401(k) plans.

4. *Time* magazine also got into the act and wrote an article on the issue – only featuring Judson and no other financial professional.

Press Release Samples

We outlined the importance of understanding what constitutes a pitch and what constitutes a press release. Not only understanding this is important, but practicing proper "press release etiquette" is mandatory. Keep in mind that journalists are inundated with materials everyday from people just like you hoping to capture their attention. Not only knowing what a press release is used for important, but knowing how they are structured is also vital.

The following release was distributed for a client regarding a national educational campaign, which fit with the timeliness criteria of the news:

 FOCUSonFiduciary™

FOR IMMEDIATE RELEASE
Contact: *Benjamin Lewis*
Perception, Inc.
301-963-7555

Consumer Financial Education Campaign Launched Nationally:
*NAPFA's **Focus on Fiduciary** campaign to educate consumers on need for Fiduciary Standards*

Arlington Heights, IL (July 1, 2006) – The National Association of Personal Financial Advisors (NAPFA), the nation's leading professional association of comprehensive, Fee-Only Financial Advisors, have officially launched a consumer-oriented, public service campaign aimed at educating Americans about the need for financial professionals to hold themselves to a Fiduciary Standard. The campaign – *Focus on Fiduciary* – will continue throughout the summer.

With the goal of making the campaign an annual occurrence, NAPFA hopes to shed light on the issues surrounding Fiduciary Standards in the financial industry while helping consumers ask the right questions of their respective Financial Advisors. To make the campaign as effective as possible, NAPFA has developed several resources available to the industry and consumers alike, including:

- An informative website with details on the Fiduciary issue (www.FocusonFiduciary.com)
- Promotional flyers and posters
- Public Service Announcements – radio and print
- A Fiduciary Questionnaire
- Various handout materials

Perfecting The Pitch by Benjamin Lewis

NAPFA is presently working with members of the media to set-up various press tours and events in major metropolitan areas, including New York, Chicago, Boston, Los Angeles, Washington, DC, Philadelphia, Dallas, Miami, and many more. With more than 1,300 members across the country, NAPFA is hoping to spread the word about eh campaign on a grassroots level.

"Financial Advisors who are held to a Fiduciary Standard will act in the client's best interests. Those who do not hold themselves to a Fiduciary Standard may be improper in their work with clients," said Peggy Cabaniss, national chair of NAPFA. "We are in no way indicating that every financial professional who operates on a Fee-Based or Commission-Only basis is going to be improper in their handling of client accounts. We do, however, believe that consumers need to understand the differences between

Financial Advisors so they can make the best decision possible when it comes to working with one. We believe the *Focus on Fiduciary* campaign will go a long way to helping consumers understand these differences."

NAPFA is distributing CD-ROMs with pre-recorded Public Service Announcements (PSA), PSA scripts, and print ads to the media throughout the summer. All PSA files are available for download through www.FocusonFiduciary.com.

Consumers and financial professionals looking for information on the *Focus on Fiduciary* campaign can visit www.FocusonFiduciary.com. Members of the media eager to work with NAPFA with regard to the campaign can contact Benjamin Lewis of Perception, Inc. at 301-963-7555 or Benjamin.lewis@perceptiononline.com.

ABOUT NAPFA

Since 1983, The National Association of Personal Financial Advisors (NAPFA) has provided Fee-Only financial planners across the country with some of the strictest guidelines possible for professional competency, comprehensive financial planning, and Fee-Only compensation. With more than 1,000 members across the country, NAPFA has become the leading professional association in the United States dedicated to the advancement of Fee-Only financial planning.

For more information on NAPFA, please visit www.napfa.org.

###

The following release was distributed for a client regarding a national survey of 401(k) participants and their attitudes about retirement, which fit with the uniqueness criteria of news. As we stated earlier in the book, original data always sells:

THE
SCARBOROUGH
GROUP, INC.
401(K) MANAGEMENT & INVESTMENT PLANNING

NEWS

FOR IMMEDIATE RELEASE

Contact: *Benjamin Lewis*
Perception, Inc.
301-963-7555

Study Shows 401(k) Participants Feel Naïve About Investing:
Participants also skeptical of internet-based advice and Social Security

Annapolis, MD (November 28, 2006) – Apparently Enron, WorldCom, and pro-longed market/economic volatility have done little to encourage 401(k) participants to become more educated and astute about their savings plan and the factors that affect it. One thing is evident; however, people are more apprehensive than ever about the viability of internet-based 401(k) advice for their retirement plan.

The 2006 401(k) Participant Survey – conducted by The Scarborough Group, Inc. in Annapolis, MD – asked 664 plan participants around the country a series of questions regarding forms of 401(k) advice, investment behavior, and levels of confidence in current and future legislative initiatives.

The survey revealed that 90% of all respondents have been naïve about investing, whether that naïveté has been constant or sporadic. On a positive note, however, is that these same participants are not over-confident in their investing abilities (73%). "Too often people mistake information for knowledge," said J. Michael Scarborough, president of The Scarborough Group. "It is refreshing to see that people, despite the amount of information that is available through the media, are not too confident in their abilities. Too often a false sense of confidence tends to lead to foolish investing mistakes."

The survey also revealed that 72% of participants would prefer to use personal management for their 401(k) plan, meaning a live advisor provides guidance for your retirement plan and also manages the assets within it. Conversely, only 20% of participants said they would prefer an internet-based form of advice. Interestingly, though, is that only 4% of participants said they would trust advice generated from an internet-based application (this number is down from 5% in 2001).

"For too many Americans, the 401(k) is the cornerstone of retirement. It is too important to retirement for people to trust electronic advice. People need the reassurance from real professionals", said Scarborough.

Perfecting The Pitch by Benjamin Lewis

With regard to Social Security people across the board are worried about its viability for the long-term. 75% of those surveyed say they are "somewhat" or "very" concerned. Only 8% say they are "somewhat" unconcerned or "not at all" concerned. "What makes this interesting is 57% of those surveyed are 51 years old or older. Obviously a significant number of those people who are at, or close to, retirement age are concerned about Social Security. This could lead to irrational investing behavior if these folks are not careful," insisted Scarborough.

Members of the media are invited to secure a copy of the **2006 401(k) Participant Survey Report**, or can arrange interviews with J. Michael Scarborough, by contacting Benjamin Lewis of Perception, Inc. at 301-963-7555 or benjamin.lewis@perceptiononline.com.

ABOUT THE SCARBOROUGH GROUP, INC.

The Scarborough Group, Inc., provides personal, unbiased, and professional investment advice and allocation management for employees participating in a company-sponsored 401(k) savings plan. The Scarborough Group's flat-fee business model has helped establish it as one of the nation's premier providers of allocation management for 401(k) participants. The Scarborough Group is a registered investment adviser with the Securities and Exchange Commission (SEC).

For more information visit www.401kadvice.com.

###

The following release was distributed for a client regarding a new book they wrote on financial planning for younger people, which fit with the relevance criteria of the news:

NEWS

FOR IMMEDIATE RELEASE

Contact: *Benjamin Lewis*
Perception, Inc.
301-963-7555

30-Something Financial Planner Releases Financial Guide for Gens X and Y:
Getting Started **creating a stir throughout the country**

Fairfax, VA (August 29, 2006) – With the end of summer comes the reopening of schools for students, but for others it simply means another completed month of work. While being thrown into the "real world" of eight-hour work days, one of the great burdens facing Generation's X and Y is the management of their finances while building a foundation for the future.

Brian T. Jones, CFP®, financial planner and vice president of Cooper, Jones & McLeland in Fairfax, VA, has authored *Getting Started: The Financial Guide For A Younger Generation* (Larstan Publishing). The book covers the spectrum of financial issues facing younger people including debt, budgeting, getting married, and having children. Speaking as an authority on financial issues, Jones is also experiencing the same financial challenges facing others in Generation's X and Y.

Jones believes his ability to relate with the market increases the book's effectiveness. "Unlike many other financial guides, this book is straightforward and written with humor and anecdotes that will resonate with 20 and 30-year-olds," said Jones. "Whether a recent college graduate is moving into an apartment or a 30-year-old is planning their wedding, *Getting Started: The Financial Guide For A Younger Generation* is designed to advise younger people as they go through different stages of their financial life."

For more information about *Getting Started: The Financial Guide For A Younger Generation*, please contact Christen Rice of Perception, Inc. at (301) 963-7555 or Christen.rice@perceptiononline.com.

ABOUT GETTING STARTED: A FINANCIAL GUIDE FOR A YOUNGER GENERATION

Written by Brian T. Jones, CFP®, a 30-something Financial Planner and vice president of Cooper, Jones & McLeland in Fairfax, VA, the book attempts to decipher the confusing financial world for those in the younger generations. Published by Larstan Publishing, *Getting Started: The Financial Guide For A Younger Generation*, is written by a financial professional who not only works in the industry, but is living through many of the same issues other 20 and 30-year-old people are living through.

For more information, please visit www.GettingStartedFinance.com.

###

Newsworthiness Checklist

Prior to distributing a pitch to the media, be sure you can answer these questions in the affirmative. There is not a need for your story to cover all of these…that may be impossible, but it does need to meet at least a couple of these items. Based on which ones you check-off, you can then focus your targeted media list.

For example, if the story you are pitching has a local angle and has a notable local figure as the spokesperson, it makes sense to pitch the story to your local market. If the story has greater appeal to your industry and contains original data, you would want to create a media list of industry writers who cover your specific issue.

See which of these criteria you can check-off for your next pitch!

- Is the story about something new?
- Is the story about something currently taking place?
- Is the story about something unusual?
- Does the story have local appeal?
- Does the story have wide appeal to consumers?
- Does the story have wide appeal to my industry?
- Is the story about strategies/tactics people can use?
- Does the story have a unique take on a larger national story?
- Does the story have appeal to a television audience (visuals)?
- Does the story make a complex issue easier to understand?
- Does the story provide original data?
- Does the story have real anecdotes to "paint a picture"?
- Can the story be offered as an exclusive?
- Does the story make a significant assumption?
- Does the story contain a notable expert/professional?

Media Contact List

Several members of the media who participated in our survey have agreed to provide you with their names and contact information in this quick Contact List. If you plan to reach out to these journalists, please remember the lessons learned in this book. They will serve you well in your public relations activities!

Name:	Lauren Young
Outlet:	BusinessWeek
Beat/Title:	Lifestyle and Personal Finance
Phone:	212-512-2495
E-mail:	lauren_young@businessweek.com
City/State:	New York, NY
Best Form of Communication:	Email
Best Time Contact (Eastern Time):	10 to 11 AM

Name:	Karin Price Mueller
Outlet:	Newark Star-Ledger
Beat/Title:	Personal Finance
Phone:	732-792-8072
E-mail:	kpmuell@optonline.net
City/State:	Manalapan, NJ
Best Form of Communication:	Email
Best Time Contact (Eastern Time):	Flexible

Name:	Paul Maxwell
Outlet:	CableFAX
Beat/Title:	Television Distribution
Phone:	303-271-9960
E-mail:	maxfax@mediabiz.com
City/State:	Lakewood, CO
Best Form of Communication:	Email
Best Time Contact (Eastern Time):	10 to 11 AM

Name:	Don Pritchard
Outlet:	KSGM-KBDZ Radio, Sun Times News Online
Beat/Title:	General
Phone:	573-883-2980
E-mail:	suntimesnews@brick.net
City/State:	Genevieve, MO
Best Form of Communication:	Email
Best Time Contact (Eastern Time):	8 to 11 AM

Name:	kirstin pires
Outlet:	Aqua Magazine
Beat/Title:	Swimming Pool/Hot Tub Business
Phone:	608-249-0186
E-mail:	kp@aquamagazine.com
City/State:	Madison, WI
Best Form of Communication:	Email
Best Time Contact (Eastern Time):	8 to 10 AM

Name:	Patrick W. Rollens
Outlet:	Midwest Real Estate News
Beat/Title:	Commercial Real Estate
Phone:	312-644-2343
E-mail:	prollens@rejournals.com
City/State:	Chicago, IL
Best Form of Communication:	Email
Best Time Contact (Eastern Time):	8 to 10 AM/1 to 5 PM

Name:	Seka Palikuca
Outlet:	Chicago Tribune
Beat/Title:	Business Executive Moves
Phone:	312-222-4241
E-mail:	spalikuca@tribune.com
City/State:	Chicago, IL
Best Form of Communication:	Email
Best Time Contact (Eastern Time):	1 to 3 PM

Name: Joanne Wojcik
Outlet: Business Insurance Newsmagazine
Beat/Title: Employer-Sponsored Health Benefits
Phone: 303-282-4260
E-mail: jwojcik@businessinsurance.com
City/State: Golden, CO
Best Form of Communication: Email
Best Time Contact (Eastern Time): 11 AM to NOON

Name: Mark J. Pescatore, PH.D.
Outlet: Government Video
Beat/Title: Professional Video Production
Phone: 561-712-1099
E-mail: MPESCATORE@CMP.COM
City/State: West Palm Beach, FL
Best Form of Communication: Email
Best Time Contact (Eastern Time): 2 to 3 PM

Name: Jerry Morehouse
Outlet: Ledger-Enquirer
Beat/Title: Senior Editor, overseeing copy desk and business reporting staff
Phone: 706-320-4422
E-mail: jmorehouse@ledger-enquirer.com
City/State: Columbus, GA
Best Form of Communication: Email
Best Time Contact (Eastern Time): 11 AM to NOON/1 to 2 PM

Perfecting The Pitch by Benjamin Lewis

Name:	Michael Gips
Outlet:	Securitiy Management
Beat/Title:	Homeland Security
Phone:	703-518-1458
E-mail:	mgips@asisonline.org
City/State:	Alexandria, VA
Best Form of Communication:	Email
Best Time Contact (Eastern Time):	10 AM to NOON/2 to 4 PM

Name:	Robert Buckley
Outlet:	WGHP-TV
Beat/Title:	Multiple
Phone:	336-821-1191
E-mail:	bob.buckley@foxtv.com
City/State:	High Point, NC
Best Form of Communication:	Email
Best Time Contact (Eastern Time):	8 to 10 AM

Name:	Chris Bishop
Outlet:	Burlington County Times
Beat/Title:	Business
Phone:	609-871-8163
E-mail:	cbishop@phillyBurbs.com
City/State:	Willingboro, PA
Best Form of Communication:	Email
Best Time Contact (Eastern Time):	1 to 2 PM

Name:	Doug Hoffacker
Outlet:	KCNC TV /CBS Denver
Beat/Title:	Assignment Editor
Phone:	303 830-6464
E-mail:	dhoffacker@cbs.com
City/State:	Westminster, CO
Best Form of Communication:	Email
Best Time Contact (Eastern Time):	10 to 11 AM

Name: Jeff Benjamin
Outlet: Crain Communications
Beat/Title: Financial Services
Phone: 989-781-4955
E-mail: jbenjamin@crain.com
City/State: New York, NY
Best Form of Communication: Email
Best Time Contact (Eastern Time): 8 to 10 AM/After 5 PM

Name: Tom Inglesby
Outlet: PhotoMedia Publishing
Beat/Title: Technology
Phone: 760-967-6161
E-mail: tom@editor7.com
City/State: San Luis Rey, CA
Best Form of Communication: Email
Best Time Contact (Eastern Time): 8 to 10 AM

Name: Rick Alm
Outlet: The Kansas City Star
Beat/Title: Business/Gaming, Tourism,
Politics
Phone: 816-234-4785
E-mail: ralm@kcstar.com
City/State: Kansas City, MO
Best Form of Communication: Email
Best Time Contact (Eastern Time): 8 AM to 5 PM

Name: Don Ruane
Outlet: The News-Press
Beat/Title: City Government
Phone: 239-344-4619
E-mail: druane@news-press.com
City/State: Cape Coral, FL
Best Form of Communication: Email
Best Time Contact (Eastern Time): 10 to 11 AM

Perfecting The Pitch by Benjamin Lewis

Name:	Beth Schwartz
Outlet:	Luxury Las Vegas Magazine
Beat/Title:	Lifestyle
Phone:	702-380-4574
E-mail:	bschwartz@reviewjournal.com
City/State:	Las Vegas, NV
Best Form of Communication:	Email
Best Time Contact (Eastern Time):	4 to 5 PM

Name:	Charles Paikert
Outlet:	Investment News
Beat/Title:	Financial Planning
Phone:	212-210-0298
E-mail:	cpaikert@ crain.com
City/State:	New York, NY
Best Form of Communication:	Email
Best Time Contact (Eastern Time):	10 AM to 5 PM

Name:	Ken Burke
Outlet:	Goldmine
Beat/Title:	Roots Music
Phone:	623-374-5664
E-mail:	driguana1@aol.com
City/State:	Canyon City, AZ
Best Form of Communication:	Email
Best Time Contact (Eastern Time):	1 to 2 PM

Name:	Hannah Smalltree
Outlet:	TechTarget/SearchDataManagement.com
Beat/Title:	Technology (data management)
Phone:	781-657-1799
E-mail:	hsmalltree@techtarget.com
City/State:	Newburyport, MA
Best Form of Communication:	Email
Best Time Contact (Eastern Time):	10 AM to NOON/1 to 3 PM

Name: Nancy Weil
Outlet: IDG News Service
Beat/Title: Editor
Phone: 617-239-7803
E-mail: nancy_weil@idg.com
City/State: Boston, MA
Best Form of Communication: Email
Best Time Contact (Eastern Time): 10 AM to NOON/2 to 3 PM

Name: Mark Mayfield
Outlet: Pro AV Magazine
Beat/Title: Commercial AV System Integration
Phone: 508-529-9390
E-mail: mmayfield@ascendmedia.com
City/State: Upton, MA
Best Form of Communication: Email
Best Time Contact (Eastern Time): 10 to 11 AM

Name: Michael Dill
Outlet: South Dade News Leader
Beat/Title: Sports, Politics, Education, Crime
Phone: 305-245-2311
E-mail: mdill@calkins-media.com
City/State: Homestead, FL
Best Form of Communication: Email
Best Time Contact (Eastern Time): 10 AM to NOON/1 to 5 PM

Name: Jeff Pfeiffer
Outlet: Tribune Media Services
Beat/Title: Entertainment/TV/Film/Music
Phone: 414-247-5053
E-mail: jpfeiffer@tribune.com
City/State: Glendale, WI
Best Form of Communication: Email
Best Time Contact (Eastern Time): 8 to 11 AM

Name: Samuel Greengard
Outlet: Freelance
Beat/Title: Business and Technology
Phone: 503-744-0132
E-mail: sam@greengard.com
City/State: West Linn, OR
Best Form of Communication: Email
Best Time Contact (Eastern Time): After 5 PM

Name: Robert Colson
Outlet: Freelance
Beat/Title: Entertainment
Phone: 615-794-5843
E-mail: robiwan@bellsouth.net
City/State: Franklin, TN
Best Form of Communication: Email
Best Time Contact (Eastern Time): 10 to 11 AM/1 to 5 PM

Name: Robert Philpot
Outlet: Fort Worth Star-Telegram
Beat/Title: Entertainment (primarily TV, also movies, radio)
Phone: 817-390-7872
E-mail: rphilpot@star-telegram.com
City/State: Edgecliff Village, TX
Best Form of Communication: Email
Best Time Contact (Eastern Time): 10 AM to NOON/2 to 5 PM

Name: Toni May
Outlet: WXEL-TV
Beat/Title: PBS - Culture, Arts, Lifestyle
Phone: 561-737-8000
E-mail: tmay@wxel.org
City/State: Boynton Beach, FL
Best Form of Communication: Email
Best Time Contact (Eastern Time): 10 AM to NOON

Name:	Nancy Eshelman
Outlet:	Patriot-News (Harrisburg, PA)
Beat/Title:	Columnist
Phone:	717-255-8163
E-mail:	neshelman@pnco.com
City/State:	Harrisburg, PA
Best Form of Communication:	Email
Best Time Contact (Eastern Time):	10 AM to NOON/1 to 4 PM

Name:	David Kronke
Outlet:	Los Angeles Daily News
Beat/Title:	TV Critic
Phone:	818-713-3638
E-mail:	davidkronke@aol.com
City/State:	Los Angeles, CA
Best Form of Communication:	Email
Best Time Contact (Eastern Time):	11 AM to NOON/1 to 5 PM

Name:	Richard Koreto
Outlet:	Wealth Manager Magazine
Beat/Title:	Financial Planning
Phone:	201-526-1254
E-mail:	rkoreto@highlinemedia.com
City/State:	Hoboken, NJ
Best Form of Communication:	Email
Best Time Contact (Eastern Time):	8 to 10 AM

Name:	Susan Nunziata
Outlet:	Entertainment Marketing Letter
Beat/Title:	Entertainment + Marketing
Phone:	212-941-1633
E-mail:	snunziata@epmcom.com
City/State:	New York, NY
Best Form of Communication:	Email
Best Time Contact (Eastern Time):	8 to 10 AM

Name:	Emma Johnson
Outlet:	MSN Money
Beat/Title:	Money, Health, Profiles
Phone:	646-346-4751
E-mail:	emma@emma-johnson.net
City/State:	Astoria, NY
Best Form of Communication:	Email
Best Time Contact (Eastern Time):	10 to 11 AM

Name:	Grace W. Weinstein
Outlet:	Freelance
Beat/Title:	Personal Finance
Phone:	201-568-4295
E-mail:	gwweinstein@compuserve.com
City/State:	Englewood, NJ
Best Form of Communication:	Email
Best Time Contact (Eastern Time):	None Given

Name:	Robert Gough
Outlet:	UCG
Beat/Title:	Energy
Phone:	301-287-2496
E-mail:	rgough@opisnet.com
City/State:	Rockville, MD
Best Form of Communication:	Email
Best Time Contact (Eastern Time):	None Given

Benjamin Lewis

With a background in political, non-profit, and financial public relations, Benjamin Lewis helps small business owners and entrepreneurs achieve a higher level of exposure and awareness. Recognized in various professional publications for public relations excellence, he shows the reader that all relationships, especially those with journalists, are built on a Foundation of Media Rapport™.

Benjamin Lewis is the Founder and President of Perception, Inc. and can be found speaking on public relations at a number of conferences across the country. He and his family reside in Maryland.

THE **FOUNDATION** OF *Media Rapport*

To learn more about the Foundation of Media Rapport™, visit www.mediarapport.com.